Rehearsal Guide
for the
Choral Director

Rehearsal Guide

for the

Choral Director

by Jack Boyd

Mark Foster
MUSIC COMPANY

Box 4012, Champaign IL, 61820

A Word
About
This Book

When I began directing high school choirs, there was no book such as this one on the market. Believe me, I looked. There were isolated chapters on rehearsal technique in several books and pamphlets, but most of them were idealistic musings on the necessity of getting something done in the rehearsal. My only recourse was to try various techniques, keeping those that worked and rejecting those that did not. This book is based on those rehearsal devices which have proved successful over the years under various conditions and with groups of widely varying abilities.

While there are a number of books aimed at amateur choruses in general and high school choruses in particular, with information on the buying of robes, lists of graded music, and related items, there is no book on the market which is specifically concerned with rehearsal problems. An analysis of the performances of the famous instrumental and vocal ensembles will reveal that the few gestures used by the conductor are only reminders of past instruction and not repeats of his actual rehearsal procedures. The work is done in the workshop, not in the show window.

This book is dedicated to the proposition that a rehearsal is a period of time which can be planned in a logical manner. With a list of the requirements of a piece of choral music plainly before him, a choral conductor should be able to design a rehearsal that will not only prepare the group for a specific performance but also instruct the singers in the art of vocal music. Both results are important, but the second is often ignored under the pressure of an impending concert. The design of this book is to take you from

5

the prerehearsal selecting of music and the planning of a year's programs, through the opening tryouts and rehearsals, up to the closing rehearsal and the time to step on stage. Its aim is to sweep away some of the terror attached to standing in front of a group wondering "What should they work on next?" Even experienced conductors find themselves getting into habits of rehearsing that limit their effectiveness. Although the beginner has no bad habits to overcome, neither does he have good habits to fall back on. This book is for both the new and the experienced conductor.

There are certain areas this book will *not* cover, such as lengthy explanations of solo vocal technique, lists of selected choral music, and designing scenery for a musical. There is no philosophy of Art (with a capital) or a history of choral music. This book is concerned with preparing a chorus and its music for proper rehearsal. Since the tryout of the chorister is in actuality the first rehearsal between director and singer, a chapter has been given over to tryout procedures. Scheduling of rehearsals is also a factor in getting a chorus ready. The chorus may wish to perform some works with instrumental accompaniment, and the techniques of instrumental rehearsal are somewhat different than vocal. There must be some sense of style in the singing, so without at least a beginning knowledge of some stylistic factors there cannot be an effective rehearsal. All of these points, and several others, are covered in this book.

One particular feature should prove quite useful: five pieces of choral music from five different periods of musical history will be examined for stylistic features and rehearsal problems. Each piece of choral music has built-in problems and advantages, particularly in contemporary music, and these problems and advantages have not been covered in previous books.

The amateur chorister needs a well-designed rehearsal to keep him from becoming bored, help him train and keep a good voice, prepare him psychologically for a coming concert, and prove to him that something is being accomplished. Every experienced choral conductor knows the problem. This book is designed to help with the answers.

JACK BOYD

Contents

Rehearsal Guide

for the

Choral Conductor

CHAPTER 1

Taking Care of Prerehearsal Necessities

The high school choral director who has been teaching in the same school for several years will be able to shorten somewhat the following list of prerehearsal "necessities," but he will eliminate them at his own risk. The director who wants a "grooved" program, meaning one that works with the least possible friction from outside forces and with the least possible work for himself, will find that the first items he rejects are those that have to do with getting the school year off to a solid start. This means he may ignore looking through the files, forget to list the coming concerts, disregard the important days which are governed by other departments, and so forth. Without this information, which must be renewed *each* year, the director will be running his department blindfolded.

Know What Is Already Available

Most schools will have a room or corner devoted to filing cabinets or shelves with the remnants of past concerts. This usually includes octavos and booklets of music, old programs, posters, and possibly some files concerning chorus personnel. It is the first order of business to plow through this morass of material, throwing away what is useless and filing the rest. Be careful, however, about throwing anything away. The memory of something desperately needed which was casually thrown away returns regularly to haunt teachers in all fields. A good rule of thumb for going to a new school may be: *don't throw anything away the first year. Just file it.*

The next move is to go through *every* choral file you have in your library. There is an emphasis on the word *every*, because only through a personal knowledge of the available music will you be able to pick out folders of music on a moment's notice for sight-reading or make up a program of three numbers for a PTA meeting scheduled five days hence. This is particularly important for the music that is in the files (with a sufficient number of copies) but which you have not personally performed.

Further, it is useful to count the octavos each time you go through the files, unless you remember positively how many copies of the work there are. Besides being a mnemonic device to force the title and composer more deeply into your mind, this counting enables you to review the works which are available for concert use and decide which ones need an additional ten or 15 copies to reach the proper number. Except in extreme cases, there should never be more than two singers to a copy of music. The reason for this is that two singers seldom hold the music at the same angle or turn the pages at the same time. Putting three or four singers on the same copy compounds the problem.

If you have only choruses of mixed voices but you find some old files of music for Soprano/Soprano/Alto (SSA) or Tenor/Tenor/Baritone/Bass (TTBB), or even two-part choral music, go through these files also. One of the problems in rehearsing and preparing a program of choral music is the ever-present threat that much of the music may turn out sounding the same. An hour and a half of straight Soprano/Alto/Tenor/Bass (SATB) music tends to turn a concert into musical oatmeal—it may be good, solid material, but it is all of the same style. The addition of two or three SSA selections and one or two Tenor/Baritone/Bass (TBB) or

TTBB numbers, can give a welcome added dimension and texture to a concert. A side benefit is that this can often be done with little or no extra cash outlay for octavos, if the music comes from the supposedly "dead" files. This will be examined in more detail in Chapter 12, "Rehearsing the All-Male and All-Female Choir."

Don't confuse this work of sorting through and counting the octavos in the files with the chores performed by your student librarian. Student help is useful for tidying up and doing menial chores, but the knowledge of the files is of no use if it is entirely in the head of some student. You should divorce yourself from mechanical tasks such as passing out music and refiling music which has been used for sight-reading or in a concert. On the other hand, only you are qualified to say if a piece of music will fit into a choral program or if it should be used for sight-reading in a rehearsal. This kind of knowledge requires dusty digging.

Which Concert Is Next?

Proper rehearsal technique demands that you know which concerts are the most pressing. It is obvious that the closest concert will be getting the most attention. This requires a full nine-month view of the choral program. Without this overall view there will be a constant scrambling for music, with the added problems which come with the students continually singing music which is not needed immediately but which through constant singing has been polished to a concert state. There is a severe psychological problem in bringing a piece of music to concert level much in advance of the concert.

First, make a list of all of the times each choral group sang the previous year, with the number of pieces performed and/or the total time allowed (or required!) for the performance. Then anticipate programs which might have been omitted from that particular year. Some schools alternate years on such observances as Flag Day, religious holidays, Memorial Day, and locally important events (founding of the city, founding of the state, local elections, and similar days). Further, keep an eye on the newspapers for upcoming celebrations which might suggest or require programs, such as the opening of a new school, a church dedication, installation of School Board members, or a state-level meeting by a civic or social group. The importance of all of these is compounded if members of the Board of Education or the school administration are active in these events. In a word: *anticipate unannounced programs.*

The following list will contain many of these events, along with the approximate timings I have found most common:

- Open house—3 numbers/10 minutes.
- PTA—3 numbers/10 minutes.
- Thanksgiving—2 or 3 numbers.
- Parents' night—3 numbers/10 minutes.
- All-state or district festival chorus—5 to 10 numbers, depending on its relative importance.
- Christmas program—any number of selections are possible if a pageant or play is involved.
- Service clubs—5 to 7 numbers/15 to 20 minutes.
- Spring concert—an hour and 15 minutes approximately, which includes the intermission.
- Easter sunrise service—2 or 3 numbers.
- Music festival or judging situation—2 or 3 numbers, with the elapsed time for all of them an important factor.
- Baccalaureate or graduation sermon—2 or 3 numbers.
- Graduation program—2 or 3 numbers.

Depending on the locality, this list can be lengthened or shortened. It is conceivable that in a predominantly Jewish area there might be a requirement for a Hanukkah service, or in a Chinese community there would be a request for something for a Chinese New Year or other similar celebration. A community with a large population from one ethnic background may wish the chorus to present some folk songs from the homeland during a celebration or festival. Casual questions over coffee can bring to light a number of possible trouble situations which will require brief programs, the word "trouble" being applicable only if you are caught unaware with an unprepared chorus.

When your list of possible programs has been completed, recopy it on a large cardboard or in a notebook so that enough space is left between each event for listing all of the music you select, *plus information about the event itself* (where, when, who to contact, and similar information). A 22″ × 26″ piece of poster board should hold an entire year's program for a single choir. The early scratch-and-erase work can be done in a notebook and then transferred to the poster board. Each choir should be organized in a similar manner. Just because a choir performs less and rehearses fewer times a week does not mean it should be any less organized.

All of the programs should be dated as soon as an exact date is available. By looking ahead, you can spot trouble times when you will be required to have a certain number of choral pieces ready but the time element is such that you cannot possibly do a presentable job. Without the Outline Chart you will find yourself going slowly berserk as the realization hits you that you have chosen the wrong music and made the wrong commitments. With the Outline Chart you can tell far enough ahead of time that trouble is inevitable. You can then either choose easier music or make arrangements for another choir to take the assignment.

It is also helpful to pencil in important dates which will involve the entire student body, such as important football or basketball games, days when the marching band will be involved (you may have several singers in the band), all-school elections, and so on.

Double Up and Even Up: Overlapping Programs

It is obvious that many numbers can be used two or more times if the audiences have little or no chance of overlapping attendance. Appearances before civic service clubs can use the same program, with the possible exception that the Rotarians and Lions might frown on a rousing rendition of "Hail Kiwanis, Club Supreme." If such club appearances occur early in December, most or all of the program might conceivably come from the music of the school assembly program. *But put such information down on the Outline Chart* so you will know how much time you have to rehearse for each concert. You might be able to begin rehearsing the music for the Spring concert before Christmas if the rehearsals are properly arranged. On the other hand, you may have problems keeping the performances fresh if you keep some numbers in the repertory from September through May. And nothing is more gauche than singing a Christmas carol on a Spring concert or for a service club in March.

The Value of Being Conservative in August

No matter how well you know your choir there are always some terrifying surprises at the first rehearsal. The father of your best accompanist was just transferred by his firm and the whole family will be leaving within the week. The only decent soprano soloist has decided to give her full time to cheerleading. These sorts of things, after they happen a few times, virtually force conservatism on a conductor.

For these and three dozen other reasons, you should choose your music to be purchased at two different times—early August and early October. The first series of purchases should be aimed at taking care of the early programs you anticipate occurring before Thanksgiving. The second series of purchases should take care of the rest of the school year, with minor exceptions, which will be taken care of by single purchases as the need arises.

The first purchases should be conservative in most technical respects. The ranges should be somewhat limited, they should not be too involved or complicated harmonically, the melodic content should be more tonally and traditionally oriented, and there should be fewer divided sections. The reason for this is simple self-preservation. There are far too many things which can happen to the choral department which cannot be controlled by the director for a haphazard, no-holds-barred choice of music. This should by no means be taken as a suggestion that trite or infantile music be selected. There are excellent choral works from all musical eras, including the twentieth century, which are technically easy. The director who deliberately forces his chorus to wade into difficult music up to its collective neck at the outset of school may find himself with ill-rehearsed singers when the first program rolls around. Since a reasonable amount of time should be given to sight-reading and vocal pedagogy for the first few weeks, judicious choosing of music for the August purchases is a must.

Since most school systems begin about Labor Day, an early October date for further music purchases should give you four or five weeks to learn the strengths and weaknesses of your new choir. After four weeks of rehearsal, you will no longer be walking blindly with a new choir. You will know if your basses can go below an F or if your tenors have an E-flat and nothing else. You will know how many rehearsal pianists you have, and whether or not any of them can play difficult scores or transpose at sight. Your soloist situation will have stabilized, with the possible exception of your tenors (who have been known to change into basses over a long weekend). This is the time to order the difficult music.

The reason for discussing the choosing and ordering of music in a book on rehearsal techniques, is that improper choice of music can upset the schedule of rehearsals so completely that the choir may never give a relaxed and confident program. A lack of rehearsal time means one of three things: the director did not budget his time properly, the director did not choose his music logically, or the director did not plan ahead.

Take Care of Those Old Charts

After the last program or during the final week of school, you should take the Outline Chart and transfer the information it contains to regular typing paper and file this information in an easily accessible place. As the years go by, you will have a permanent file which will show which pieces of music have been performed by which groups. This will keep the PTA from hearing the same version of "Red River Valley" every year for four consecutive years.

The first-year director will not have the experience to see at a glance that a piece of music is better placed later in the year. For this basic reason, the first-year director must adhere to a well-formed and detailed Outline Chart from the very beginning.

The Physical Plant: Odds and Ends

Check the piano! It may take a few weeks to get the best piano technician to put it in working shape. A beginning rehearsal without a piano in top working order can be a very awkward and embarrassing time. Don't wait until the first rehearsal to discover that the middle octave is a total disaster area.

Clean the chalkboards and take down old bulletin board material. The first rehearsal must be the beginning of something new, not the interrupted continuation of the previous year. Particularly is this important for the new teacher in his first year with a school system. A beginning rehearsal is part physical and part psychological. Anything which minimizes the excitement of a new beginning (or which reminds the students of last year's director) should be eliminated.

Check the recording equipment, both tape and record. It may take several days to get the equipment in proper working condition. Also, if you have a student with a talent in the area of electronics, now is the time to instruct him in the operation of all equipment so when rehearsal time comes he will be ready to play or record as needed. The use of student help will speed up the rehearsal since you can continue directing while your engineer gets ready, and then you can resume rehearsing as he locks up the equipment. Tape-recording a rehearsal or listening to another performance of a piece can be quite valuable, but not if it takes an unreasonable chunk of the rehearsal period. It is obvious that such a job does not require a student with a keen musical ear. A student with more enthusiasm than vocal talent might be persuaded that he is more valuable as a recording engineer than as a participating singer.

Folders for the Students

Far too much time is lost with the physical mechanics of getting the music in front of the singers. Methods of initial distribution will be discussed later. One of the prerehearsal necessities will be making sure that a sufficient supply of choral folders of some type are available from the first rehearsal on. There are a number of styles available, the two most common being: (1) those with pockets which expand to hold up to 15 or 20 average-size octavos; and (2) those with some type of string, elastic, or metal wire which holds approximately a dozen average-size octavos ready for rehearsing or concert. The first type is more quickly organized but harder to control in either a concert or a rehearsal, since the single octavo to be used must be retrieved from a handful of octavos. On the other hand, the second type of folder takes longer to "load" and "unload" but the music is ready at hand and always in the same order (if the singers are instructed to place the pieces in a certain order). One method of eliminating some of the pawing through the pocket-style folder is to keep all of the sacred selections on one side and the secular on the other, or the music for the closest concert can be on one side and future concert music on the other. This is somewhat idealistic, however, since the music tends to become mixed quite easily.

Another solution is to use both types of folders—the pocket type at first while sight-reading or trying several different works, then when a program or concert is in its final stages the selected works can be placed in the concert folders in the proper order. This has the added benefit of cutting wear and soiling to a minimum on the folders used in concert.

There is always the problem of where to keep the folders. A simple set of pigeonholes, one for each folder, is the best. This is also helpful in distributing the music since one copy can be placed in each pigeonhole by the librarian before the folders are picked up. Music to be returned to the library can either be handed in by the entire choir, or it can be taken from the folders and placed outside of them in the pigeonholes.

Standing, Seated, or Leaning

Whether the choir stands or sits for rehearsal is often determined by the physical area in which the practice takes place. If the rehearsal must be conducted in a room which is normally used for some other purpose when the choir is not rehearsing (gym classes or cafeteria), then setting up or taking down risers or rearranging chairs or tables may be the final determinant. However, in those schools with a separate room for choral rehearsal there is usually some type of built-in series of risers.

The style of chair selected can have a pronounced effect on both the sound and the attitude of the singers. The average type of folding chair with the back slightly reclined is probably the worst kind to use. Basically it is far too comfortable. While discomfort is not the main goal of a rehearsal, nevertheless, a comfortable chair holds a very large temptation for the singer to lean back and relax all of the muscles which should not be relaxed while singing. Instrumentalists know of this temptation and often request chairs with flat seats and straight backs. These can give some support to the singer's back while he is resting during the playing or singing by another section.

The opposite of this is the use of standing risers during the entire rehearsal. This has the effect of getting the singers used to standing for extended periods, which is valuable when the time comes for a lengthy concert. It also has the negative effect of gradually accumulated fatigue during an hour rehearsal. A two-hour, on-riser rehearsal would be unthinkable.

A middle ground is the use of stools with an approximately 30-inch high seat. The stools should not have backs, as are sometimes shown on the popular home-style barstools. The stools are only to be used to lean against, not to sit on. Because of the height there is less of a tendency to slump than in the more common 18- or 19-inch height of school chairs. When one section is not singing those singers can sit on the stools, but they can slip into proper singing position in an instant.

CHAPTER 2

Preparing the
Director's Score

As soon as the music has been ordered and begins arriving, you need to begin assembling your Director's Folio. This consists of all of the choral music and all of the sight-reading material you will be needing for the first week or two of rehearsals. In addition, it is helpful to have a list of personnel (as soon as it is available) and a descriptive list of the first few programs, including the selections to be performed. There should also be a brief outline of things you want to discuss *at the end of the first rehearsal* (don't begin with explanations or discussions; the singers have come to sing).

The purpose of the Director's Folio is to provide, in a single spot, everything you will need for one complete rehearsal. The sight of a director constantly running back to his office to get a piece of music, or a baton, or some list is not calculated to prove to the singers that the director is a well-organized leader. A rehearsal, if it is properly designed, goes in a straight line from beginning to end with no time out for the singers to become interested in conversations or nonmusical goings-on. The use of the Director's Folio and regular prerehearsal organization will virtually eliminate these deviations.

23

The Folio Itself

This can take two forms: (1) a portfolio type of container which has dividers so that different types of material can go in separate sections; or (2) a loose-leaf notebook with several dividers. Although it is easier to put the octavos in proper order the first time in a portfolio, it is more difficult to keep them in the proper order.

At various times I have used each type, and the second type —the loose-leaf notebook—has worked the best. It should be a good quality three-ring notebook with 1½-inch rings. This size is preferable to the standard 1-inch rings because of the larger number of pages it will take. Also, the added area within the rings themselves keeps the edges of the pages from jamming together and allows them to turn more easily. On a concert with 20 or 25 octavos, this jamming can present a problem. Also, for some unknown reason, the holes do not tear as readily when the larger rings are used.

The octavos which will be performed (as distinct from those which will merely be sung through once or twice and then returned to the files) should be cut at the fold and then punched with a three-hole punch. This should be a standard piece of equipment for a choral department since it can also be used for punching the holes for sight-reading sheets, dittoed or mimeographed manuscript music, or any other printed material you wish the students to keep. Obviously, if the portfolio is used, there will be no need to cut or punch the octavos. When refiling, simply staple the cut octavo.

As the octavos are cut and punched (and reinforcements placed on the holes), they should go in the Folio according to the program or concert coming up, the more immediate pieces nearer the front, the later ones farther back. If the pieces for more than one program are being worked on at one time and a program comes up, it is only logical to take the ones for the immediate program and put them in a section by themselves so that no confusion arises on the actual program. The final rehearsal should find these pieces in the proper order and in a predictable place in the Director's Folio. Having this Folio ready for the final rehearsal helps eliminate lost motion and helps "groove" both the program and the director. Anything strange happening on the program adds just that much needless tension. Accidentally turning to the wrong piece, forgetting the name of the next number, or any of a dozen things can happen. This will be covered more thoroughly in Chapter 15, "Judging When a Choral Work Is Ready for Performance."

The next section of the Folio should contain the sight-reading sheets or other material for interval and rhythm training. Near the end of the year this may not be used as much and will probably be taken from the Folio, but at the beginning of the year it will be a prominent part of each rehearsal.

Finally, there will be a section which will hold such information as student personnel lists, a list of the upcoming programs and their requirements, student assignments (librarian, room monitor, program chairman, robe or uniform chairman, officers, etc.), and possibly all of the information normally carried on the Outline Chart. If an actual chart is not used, all of the information should be kept in the Director's Folio.

If you direct more than one choir you may want to have a separate section in the Director's Folio for each choir, or you may find that a separate Folio for each choir is handier. Only trial and error will give you this information.

Color Coding

A score is only as useful as the information it contains. The purpose of color coding your director's score is to: (1) make more obvious the information already there; and (2) insert your own deductions as to the proper interpretation of the music.

These two areas require two different styles of marking. In the first area it is easiest to use a felt-tipped "highlighter" type of marker so important interpretative markings are immediately obvious. I prefer yellow because it seems to allow the black printing to stand out in greater relief than the other pastel colors, and it contrasts well with the red pencil used for other markings. The yellow highlighter is used on the following items, among others:

- Tempo markings (adagio, poco allegro).

- Metronome markings (♩ = 72).

- All time changes.
- All key changes.

- Musica ficta.

- Accent marks (> ∨ <)

- Articulation marks.
- Section letters or numbers.
- Tempo or dynamic changes (accelerando, crescendo, etc.).
- Unusual words, word endings, or prefixes (plurals, foreign words, unusual or obsolete English words).

In other words, everything that is on the printed page which is designed to help you interpret the music correctly should have the highlighter applied to it. This could even include some part of an introductory statement or Editor's Notes if there is some particularly important information which you need to recall periodically or which you want to call to the attention of the singers. It is conceivable that the composer's, arranger's, author's, or editor's name, or even the date of publication or the publishing firm, could be important enough to warrant highlighting.

The second part of color coding involves the use of a colored pencil which will contrast with the highlighter. This is used for all other markings in your interpretation of the work. This will include:

- Breath marks (for the full chorus or one section).
- "No breath" marks (commonly called a "carry-over").
- Tempo or dynamic markings where there are none printed.
- Anticipated melodic or harmonic problems (particularly non-diatonic patches of melody).
- Unusual word problems or anticipated problems.

- Important cues for nonmusic events governed by the music itself (lights, entrances, etc.).

A colored pencil is suggested rather than a marking pen, because these are the areas which are often modified as you progress through the rehearsing of a piece. You may wish to change the breathing markings or adjust the dynamics according to the acoustics of your particular concert hall or the strength of your choir (or one section of your choir). A *colored* pencil is suggested because it is more easily noticed in glancing at the score. I prefer a red pencil because it shows up well and contrasts with the yellow highlighter.

There is this one basic admonition: *don't overmark your score at first.* Make only those marks which will help you through the first one or two rehearsals. Further study of the score will show you new trouble spots, and further rehearsal will turn up anticipated trouble spots which were easily negotiated. As soon as possible, clean up the score by erasing useless markings. There is no need to be reminded at the time of the concert of difficult areas which have long since been solved.

Looking for Trouble Spots

Trouble spots fall into four categories: (1) music, (2) text, (3) interpretative markings, and (4) style problems. The last named, isolating and applying stylistic concepts, will be covered more thoroughly in Chapter 7, "Developing Proper Choral Tone and Style in the Rehearsal." The other three deserve individual attention.

Vocal music, much more than instrumental music, is influenced by traditional musical writing procedures. A clarinet can negotiate almost any type of disjointed melody, as long as it stays within the possible range of the instrument. A voice, on the other hand, has a tendency to translate everything into a diatonic scale context. This is particularly frustrating to many contemporary composers who may have little acquaintance with voices and insist on writing long stretches of nondiatonic music. This is no indictment of the composer, who must follow his Muse wherever

27

it leads him. However, it is necessary for you, as a director, to spot these rocky stretches of nondiatonic music and adequately analyze and mark them so the rehearsal can be as valuable as possible.

Pre-1900 vocal music had very few of these troublesome melodic spots, since music was still controlled by traditional voice leading and tonality. Post-World War I saw composers "playing against the scene" with more use of nonpredictable melodies and harmonies. It is the areas in a composition which are nonpredictable that will receive the heaviest red pencilling. Such things as cross-relations (a natural and altered form of a note, either simultaneously or consecutively), sudden time or key changes, notes concerning tuning problems or opportunities (octaves or fifths providing points of tonal reference), and other such items which will come to light as you go through a score should be marked.

Be sure not to make the markings too elaborate. A breath mark can be a simple slash mark after a note or a word. A carryover is the same marking as a phrase marking, just a simple curved line connecting two notes or two words. A chord or interval which has a strategic usefulness or a problem should have a simple rectangle drawn around it. Cues should not use sentences, but rather one- or two-word reminders such as "lights," "choir enters," or "chimes begin." The markings are only for reminding you of problems you encountered in your studying of the score, not complete sentences describing the battlefield. If a more elaborate explanation is desired, as for instance in the description of an involved articulation problem, then draw a line to the top or bottom of the page and write abbreviated sentences in very small printing.

It will take a few weeks for you to devise your own set of markings if you do not already have a set in use. The markings do not have to conform to those suggested in this chapter, but they: (1) must be consistent, and (2) must be clear at a glance.

Final Color Coding

As the program or concert approaches, it may be apparent that some more information needs to be available to you. Such things as names of soloists or accompanists, notes about important aspects of the piece you want to tell the audience, if the chorus is about to change position on stage, and similar information, should be noted in a third contrasting color, possibly green. It is all too easy to forget names and other information under the pressure of being in front of an audience. Be sure, however, not to put this extramusical information in the same color as the musical information, and don't put it where it will interfere with the reading of the music itself.

What NOT to Put in Color

Take care that you do not, in a spasm of enthusiasm, overdo the color coding. Some contemporary composers have overdone their manuscripts to the extent that they are much more confusing than if standard musical calligraphy were used. Those things which are obvious need not be marked. Don't bother marking key signatures if only the one key is used throughout. Don't mark time signatures unless there is a change after the beginning. Mark only enough on the score to provide you with a thorough rehearsal and not so much that the score becomes a work of tinted beauty in its own right.

When a particular work has been performed and you do not anticipate any further performances, remove it from your Conductor's Folio, staple all of the pages together (you may have removed some blank pages or other extraneous pages to cut down on the bulk of the Folio), and file them in a folder marked "Conductor's Scores." Even if the student copies have been retrieved and filed in the shelves, be sure to keep your Conductor's Score readily available in case an emergency occurs and you have to pick out three or four numbers for a fast program. Having them all in one place helps overcome the problem of remembering just exactly what is available. At the end of the year, it is only a matter of a few moments' work to file them in the proper place with the rest of the copies.

A final suggestion for preparing the Folio for a concert: *check to see if there are any extra pages which need to be clipped together or removed entirely from the Folio.* These would be either blank pages or front pages which are needlessly bulky, or they might be sections of a long work which will not be performed on that particular concert. The problems involved with leafing through several unused sections to find the proper place can be eliminated by the judicious use of paper clips. These should be placed on the unused sections before the first rehearsals are begun. There is no more defense for wasting time turning pages during a rehearsal than during a concert.

CHAPTER 3

Running the
Choral Tryout

The tryout is *not* to show the student who is running the choral department. The tryout is *not* to prove that the student knows less than the director.

Basically, the purpose of the tryout is to place the student with some ability in the proper section and to give the director some basis for judging both the present state and the anticipated future progress of the singer's voice. It is obvious that without the proper singers there can be only an inept chorus. This does not mean every singer must be well trained before being added to the chorus, but it does mean he or she must have some innate ability both in singing and in hearing music. Further, the director must know a minimum amount about each voice for proper placement within the chorus and within each section of the chorus.

The Biographical Sheet

This is a mimeographed or dittoed sheet which gives basic biographical information at the top of the page, the bottom of the page being reserved for comments by the director during the tryout. These sheets should be distributed to the singers some time

INFORMATION SHEET

Abilene Christian College Choral Department

Name _____ Class _____

Abilene address _____ Major subject _____

Home address _____

Brief list of high school choral activities _____

_____

_____

_____

Brief list of college choral activities _____

_____

_____

_____

Other vocal activities (voice lessons, operetta, folk singing, church chorus, etc. _____

_____

_____

What instrument(s) do you play, and how long? _____

Will you play in the band or orchestra? _____

Are you on academic probation? _____

- 0 - 0 - 0 - 0 - 0 - 0 - 0 - 0 -

SR: int _____

SR: rh _____

Ph rep _____

V Q _____

Com _____

_____

(left margin, vertical) Assignment

(left margin) ×

Figure 3–1

before the tryout itself so they may be filled out and handed to the director at the beginning of the tryout.

A number of items have proven helpful to a proper understanding of a prospective singer's true level of ability. Besides the predictable name, address, telephone number, age, and grade, the following information will be useful on the high school level:

- Parents' occupations.
- How long in this school system?
- Describe previous school choral work.
- Describe previous church or other choral work.
- What instruments do you play, and how long for each?
- Will you play in the band or orchestra?
- Describe extracurricular plans for this year.
- Post-high school plans.

Without this information before him, the director will find it difficult to properly evaluate the student and the voice. A student who has studied violin for six years should sight-read better than a student who has studied voice for only one year. Thus, if the violin student consistently sings off-pitch it is a more critical problem than if the voice student sings incorrectly. The biographical information will cut down the subjectivity when judging the various voices.

The problem of extracurricular organizations and their attendant demands on the students' time is not so critical with a large group, but with a small chamber chorus or madrigal group it is quite important. At a showdown between singing for a PTA meeting or leading the cheers for a basketball game, guess which will get the students' nod?

At the bottom of the biographical sheet there should be separate lines with the following headings at the beginning of each line:

- Sight-reading: interval.
- Sight-reading: rhythm.
- Phrase repetition.
- Voice quality and range.

33

The average high school voice will not require a further breakdown of descriptions, since the director's job is to train and not merely organize a perfect chorus. The chart is for generalities and not for detailed criticism. If something is particularly good or bad, such as intonation, breath control, vibrato, or pronunciation, brief notes about these will be a normal part of the critique. Finally, there should be two or three empty lines for comments by you.

The General Meeting

It has been found that, if time and circumstances permit, it is quite helpful to have a general meeting of all those who wish to try out for the chorus or choruses. A series of two or three meetings is an even better idea, since this enables the singers to become more thoroughly acquainted with the director, and of equal importance, you can become acquainted with them. During this time you can demonstrate the tryout procedure, sing the tryout song a couple of times, teach the students the warm-up exercises, and generally make the tryout somewhat less fearful than it might be.

This general meeting, regardless of its length, must be structured as carefully as any rehearsal so that no time is lost. Gaps and dead places in these early meetings might discourage the already fainthearted or half-converted. In each meeting, the group should be warmed up using the same exercises which will be used for the individual tryouts. Then one or two simple sight-reading exercises (*not* the ones which will be used at the tryout, but similar to them) should be sung to reacquaint the singers with sight-reading, if they have been away from it for a few weeks or months. This will also help those who have never sight-read vocally to overcome a feeling of total helplessness at the tryout itself.

Finally, two or three *simple* choral works should be sung and very briefly polished. The goal is not performance quality but relaxation, with you as a conductor and teacher. Choose pieces which have a fair amount of unison or two-part singing at this stage. This is much easier to sight-read and gives more confidence to the singing.

34

Interval Repetition

This will be the shortest of the various segments of the try-out. It consists of brief four- or five-note sequences of progressive difficulty. The purpose is to find the degree of melodic retention. Beginning with a series of major, minor, augmented, and diminished triads, the exercises progress to virtually atonal melodies. The following illustration shows a typical series of exercises:

Interval Repetition for Tryout

Figure 3–2

Only eight or ten sequences will be needed to explore thoroughly the singer's ability. Keep the exercises within the general range of the voice for the first three or four exercises. The final two or three may go further afield by two or three octaves, with the singer echoing the melody in the most comfortable range. Each should be played only once, the possible exceptions being the final one or two most difficult exercises.

Sight-Reading

The purpose of the sight-reading tryout is to isolate those singers who cannot follow the line of the music. If the biographical sheet indicates at least a modest background in choral singing but the sight-reading level is so low as to be nonexistent, the director can only surmise that the student has a low capacity for musical achievement—or, the student is lazy. Either problem would make the student questionable choral material. Hopefully, a training chorus will be available for such a student.

The Sight-Reading Sheet consists of about ten very brief single lines of music in various keys but without words. Each part of the tryout should be specifically concerned with one part of the singer's art. Concentrate on the melody in one exercise, on rhythm in another. The first exercise should be brutally simple, with a range of no more than a fifth and preferably centered between the root and fifth of a major key. The exercises for sight-reading, as with the interval repetition, become progressively more difficult until the final exercises are using large intervals and awkward time changes. A certain amount of well-prepared chromaticism could be used, but only enough to test understanding and not enough to confuse.

You should make up a new set of exercises each year unless extreme security measures are taken with the master set. The word *set* is used to denote the two copies needed, one for you and one for the singer. The following illustration is only an example of the type of exercise progression. This one should be used only for practice (Figure 3–3).

No effort was made to create exercises which are models of melodic splendor. Rather they were devised to show off the singer's sight-reading ability. *Do not use an established melody.* The goal is to see if the singer can handle new material. These exercises may be sung on the neutral vowels *loo* or *la,* or with *sol-fa* syllables or numbers, whichever the singer feels is the easiest.

If a singer trots through an exercise with ease, you should skip the next exercise to get at a more difficult one. The entire set

36

Sight-Reading Tryout Sheet

Figure 3–3

should almost never be used. Four or five will tell you what you want to know.

The tone quality displayed during the sight-reading session should be noted carefully because this is probably the most natural sound the singer will make. That does not mean the best or the most relaxed, but the one which he commonly uses while singing without pressure. This is, of course, not always true, since the solo singing itself as well as the excitement of the tryout may generate enough adrenaline to create artificial tremors where there normally are none.

The Voice Itself

The opening warm-up session of running a few basic scales, the interval drill, and the sight-reading should have eliminated some of the pressure so the voice will be somewhat settled. The final part of the tryout is the examination of the singing voice apart from the technical problems of reading the music.

For this, a moderately simple and familiar song should be used which can be accompanied by you with simple chords. I have used "My Country, 'Tis of Thee," for choruses from junior high through college with good results. The melody is less than an octave, the words are familiar, and the chord structure makes transposition easy. Memorizing this piece in the keys of D, F, and A should cover any voice for a tryout. It will also allow each voice to perform in various keys to show off the different ranges. A copy of the words should be available for the singer in the event he does not quite remember them.

Other Tryout Procedures

Some directors use tone quality as a basis for choosing members of their choruses. This type of tryout is accomplished by having all those trying out memorize a very simple four-part hymn or song. Then a quartet of experienced voices begin, with other quartets added or subtracted until a thoroughly integrated sound is arrived at. This can also be done on a section basis with one voice beginning and individual voices from that voice classification being added until the desired sound is reached.

The advantages of this method are obvious, but so are the disadvantages. On the plus side is the ready-made tone quality. Much less time will be needed to obtain a homogeneous sound. However, this should not be considered too much of an advantage, since one sound will not work with every piece of choral music. A Marenzio motet normally requires a different tone quality than a Brahms folk song arrangement or a dissonant contemporary piece.

A distinct disadvantage is the lack of emphasis on basic musicianship from each singer, unless this has been previously determined and only the accomplished sight-readers are being considered. If only the tone quality is considered, and this under the pressure of singing before peers, a quite limited chorus is liable to result. My own experience is that the disadvantages of this procedure far outweigh the advantages.

How Much to Demand or Forgive

One of the fundamental reasons for a tryout of more than five minutes is that such a length of time allows the excess adrenaline to drain away so the most normal vocal sound can come out. In the early stages of the tryout the singer will fluster easily, become embarrassed, or possibly in extreme cases freeze altogether. In the sight-reading section, a general rule is to accept what is done correctly and ignore what is wrong (unless *everything* is wrong). Allow the singer to perform what he can perform best. The goal is to see what *can* be done, not what *cannot* be done.

Outline of a Tryout

Assuming that no general meeting has taken place, the following will be the normal series of events in a tryout.

1. A very brief and friendly greeting, then a rapid perusal of the biographical sheet to get the approximate level of attainment (½ minute).
2. Warm-up exercises which are quite simple and have a range of about a fifth. Some false starts may be anticipated. Use both staccato and legato singing (1 minute).
3. Interval drill and phrase repetition to determine aural sensitivity. Play each exercise one time only, except for the final one or two exercises (1½ minutes).

4. Sight-read four or five examples from a prepared sheet but preferably not from an octavo (keep everything as simple as possible). Play arpeggio to give the key, then play the opening note (2 minutes or less).
5. Sing a familiar and easy song or hymn, transposing as necessary to find the extent of the singer's range and the sound of the voice in various ranges (2 minutes or more).
6. Dismiss the singer and make brief notes about *all* aspects of the student's voice and musicianship. Personality quirks should also be noted (2 to 3 minutes).

A thorough tryout such as this requires at least ten minutes, six or seven minutes for the actual tryout and two or three minutes for the comments. This ten-minute period should be sufficient, including the time to come in and leave the room. Sometimes less time is needed, particularly for the advanced student or a singer you have had in your choir for two years or more. In this case, the more elementary interval drills and sight-reading examples can be omitted, as well as the chitchat designed to put the singer at ease. However, it might be well to give more time to judging the tone quality of the voice itself, since the soloists normally come from the ranks of the more experienced singers.

Ten minutes is not an excessive amount of time. A school with 500 students will probably have about 100 students try out for the choir program. At ten minutes per student, it is still less than 20 hours of tryouts. If the choral program is quite popular and 200 or more students appear for the tryout, a shorter sequence must be arranged which would consist of the following:

1. Greeting and warm-up, 1 minute.
2. Interval drill, 1 minute.
3. Sight-reading, 1 minute.
4. Familiar song, 1 minute.
5. Notes and evaluation, 1 minute.

Using this abbreviated tryout may necessitate some call-backs for the doubtful voices. However, there are always some novice singers whose destination is obvious, they have either very good or very poor voices, or their ears are quite good or made of tomato cans. If there is a second chorus for training purposes, your job is greatly simplified.

It may be possible to try out some of the voices in the Spring at the end of school. While this works with girls' voices, it is less effective with boys' voices, unless they are already completely changed. This problem notwithstanding, breaking up the tryout into Spring and Fall sessions helps alleviate the many hours of tryouts at the beginning of school.

Some schools, particularly the smaller ones, require the choral director to accept every student who wishes to sing. Without commenting on such pedagogical concepts, it is understandable when a director in this sort of position is something less than wildly enthusiastic about extensive tryouts. However, tryouts have their place even in this sort of situation, since only in this way will the director be able to properly classify voices and spot voices with flaws in technique. It will also turn up potential soloists as well as prospects for a select chorus or chamber chorus, which the director may wish to organize later in the year.

The Organization Behind the Tryout

There are certain problems which may occur in the tryout sequence which can be alleviated with a bit of pretryout planning. One is in the condition of the sight-reading sheet. If you prepare your own, be sure to spend extra time on the manuscript copy which will be used by the students. Smudged notes, obscure ledger lines, naturals and sharps which appear the same, omitted flags on eighth and sixteenth notes, omitted dots and bar lines, and many other potential pitfalls to the student singer should be attended to so he or she does not have to ask about a problem area. It is confusing to attempt reading a measure in 4/4 which has only 3½ beats in it.

The sign-up sheet is simply a paper with different times of the day listed and a blank line right after the time indicated where the student signs his name. The most common error in tryouts is for the director to attempt to squeeze in more students than he can handily try out. Always leave at least a five-minute segment at the end of each hour to take care of getting a drink, answering questions, or getting back on schedule.

Attached to the sign-up sheet should be a brief listing of the requirements or elements in a tryout. Don't try to explain everything, but merely outline the basic steps. This is for the student who just happens by and is curious. You also might include a list of the first few concerts and programs, possibly those for the first semester or all of the pre-Christmas programs so the prospective singers will know what they are getting into. Finally, in large type, let everyone know the date and time of the first rehearsal.

Have someone in the outer office to answer questions, guide newcomers to the sign-up sheet, and keep impatient students from knocking on the door to ask if it is their time yet. One of last years' singers would be best, since this person would know the tryout procedures and could answer most questions concerning the tryout and the school year's activities.

CHAPTER 4

Solving the Problems of Rehearsal Scheduling

A rehearsal at 8:00 in the morning must be structured in a different manner than one which occurs at 3:30 in the afternoon. A rehearsal 25 minutes in length must be differently organized than one 90 minutes in length. A chorus meeting once a week has different rehearsal requirements than a chorus meeting daily. Also, each of these rehearsal schedules influences both the choice of music and the number and length of programs possible in a school year.

Problems of the Before-School Rehearsal

For six years I had a select chorus which met at 8:00 A.M. each school day for a 35-minute rehearsal. Without qualification I can say there is no more ghastly sound than grouped adolescent voices at 8:00 in the morning, unless it might be those same voices at 5:30 in the morning warming up for an Easter sunrise service.

It quickly became apparent that a slower and more lengthy warm-up period was needed than for the choruses which met later in the day. But as the warm-ups increased, interest decreased. The singers did not want to take five minutes warbling repetitive and boring vocalises.

This problem was solved by the use of sight-reading exer-

Figure 4–1

cises which were changed every day or two. The exercises were extremely simple, so there was no complete concentration on notes to the detriment of vocal production, but still a considerable amount of ear-training was imparted. Figure 4–1 shows some excerpts from those early warm-up/sight-reading exercises.

They were tonal at the beginning, but as reading ability increased so did the amount of dissonance between the two voices. Each line remained diatonic but the two lines did not necessarily blend harmonically (in the traditional sense of harmonic correctness). The range seldom exceeded an octave and there were very few rhythmic intricacies in the sight-reading material designed for the warm-up period. Figure 4–2 shows one of the later atonal warm-ups.

Figure 4–2

No attempt was made to develop these exercises into triumphs of choral writing: they were designed for a specific purpose, to get rid of "morning mouth" in the least objectionable manner and train ears at the same time. The pieces written purely for sight-reading experience, and particularly for rhythm-training, were used later in the rehearsal.

These warm-up/sight-reading pieces were also used for choruses meeting later in the day, but the length of time they were used in each rehearsal was shorter. The voices had been partially warmed up by speaking and the body muscles were more under control, so the emphasis was on sight-reading/ear-training and not on warming up the voices. When the emphasis was on warming up the voice, the articulation was usually changed from example to example—first legato, then staccato, then piano, then forte. Sometimes quarter notes were divided into two eighth notes or into four sixteenth notes. Occasionally they would be sung as if they were in a different key; that is, the notes remained on the same lines or spaces but the key signature was changed from, say, two flats to three sharps. This threw all of the relationships into a different focus. We even, on occasion, sang the pieces backward!

Four or five minutes was found to be enough time for early morning warm-ups, if the pieces chosen for rehearsal immediately following the warm-up period had no extensive range problems. Rhythm was seldom a problem, unless the students were sleepy. This is another reason for warm-ups which require concentration, the minds have to be warmed up as well as the voices. Although the time allotted to sight-reading for choruses meeting later in the day gradually lessened from five or six minutes to only two or three minutes as the semester passed, the early morning rehearsal constantly required a long time for warming up.

The outline for the 35-minute morning rehearsal was as follows:

- 5 minutes for warm-up/sight-reading.
- 5 to 10 minutes rehearsal of work with limited ranges.
- The remainder unlimited rehearsal, ending with a more or less exciting piece.

Further sight-reading could come any time after the limited-range pieces were finished.

A rehearsal of less than 25 minutes has a built-in problem of not enough time left over after the voices are shaped up. It is possible to jump into a rehearsal with little or no warm-up, but the consequences will be that students wind up with hoarse voices and tight muscles, straining to hit notes by throat muscle alone. If you, as a conductor, have a 25-minute rehearsal before school, explain to the principal that in actuality you have less than a 19-minute rehearsal.

46

The After-School Rehearsal

A different problem enters with an after-school rehearsal. There is not the problem of getting the voice in shape after a night of relaxation, but the opposite problem of overcoming a day of talking and shouting. In addition, there is fatigue. Most high schools have six hours of classwork. The afternoon chorus has to overcome the psychological longing to get out of school and relax over a milk shake, and still there is a necessity to get the voice in some kind of decent singing shape.

A compromise must be reached between what is physically needed and what is psychologically needed. A bare minimum of vocal exercise should be used before getting into an exciting or emotional work. For three years I had a large afternoon chorus which met once a week to prepare an extended work for a concert. The year we prepared Brahms' *German Requiem* it became standard procedure to follow about two minutes of warm-up exercises with "Behold, All Flesh Is as the Grass." The choral part of this movement begins very low in unison, then the phrase is repeated in octaves (compound octaves), and quite soon there is the passage "Now therefore, be patient, O my brethren" which is almost a waltz. It was, from a psychological standpoint, ideal for getting the students alive and mentally on their toes. The low unison section was practically a continuation of the warm-up exercises. If we had begun on a solemn passage in a high range, such as the concluding movement "Blessed Are the Dead Which Die in the Lord" the entire rehearsal would have died the death.

Similarly, the year we performed Mendelssohn's *Elijah* the opening chorus after the warm-up period was often "Behold! God the Lord Passed By," with its abrupt change from E minor to E major. The Fauré *Requiem* was more difficult, since the entire work is serene and almost without a musical climax. However, shortly after the baritone solo in "Libera Me" the chorus has an explosive "Dies Illa" after a brief, gentle "Tremens."

One oddity which became obvious after a few rehearsals was that afternoon rehearsals could end with a "down" chorus rather than a loud, exciting explosion of sound. More often than not in the Brahms work this was the familiar "How Lovely Is Thy Dwelling Place," in *Elijah* it was "He Watching Over Israel," and almost any chorus in the Fauré *Requiem* would work. This was in direct contrast with the early morning rehearsals which seemed to want to end with an exciting number to give the chorus members a push into the day's work.

Night Rehearsals: Compounded Problems

Although night rehearsals are standard for civic and church choirs, these rehearsals for high school students present problems which may outweigh the advantages. The students' voices are generally in good shape since the dinner hour has allowed both the voices and muscles to relax. Usually there will be a large block of time for rehearsal, possibly two hours total, which would not be available during a daytime rehearsal.

On the other hand, this is a time when the students would normally be doing something else, so there is a tendency to want to talk and fraternize more than would be common during a class period or even before or after school. There is also the problem of getting both administrative and parental permission for either a one-shot meeting or a continuing series of night rehearsals. Finally, there is no night which will not have conflicts for a smaller or larger number of students. Monday and Tuesday nights are the least "conflicted." Wednesday and Thursday nights are usually for church choirs, and weekend nights are out of the question. For two years I directed a high school choir on Monday evenings from 7:00 until 9:00, and the list of excuses the students gave for not attending the rehearsals gives one immoderate pride in the inventiveness of American youth.

The organization of such night rehearsals is complicated somewhat, in that two hours is a long time to rehearse without a break for the singers. You will want to give them a break of some sort, but not so much that they will lose the impetus gained in the first hour. One method which worked well was to stagger breaks by boys and girls, so that while one group was taking a break the other group was having a part rehearsal. Then the roles were reversed for the next 15 minutes. Part rehearsals are quite valuable, and generally after 45 minutes you know of enough places which need specialized work that you can take the time without feeling you are wasting the time of the rest of the class. If the work or works are far enough into being rehearsed, you may be able to schedule specific pages for part rehearsals before the actual rehearsal begins.

The benefits of the staggered break are obvious: part rehearsals are taken care of, only half as many are trying to get to the water fountains, and there is no break in the continuity of the rehearsal. It is understood that you, the director, will have no break as such, only enough time to grab a drink while the full group is reassembling. If you wish, you may eliminate even that lost time by having a student bring you a glass of water.

The outline of the rehearsal, except for the break, will be much like that of any other rehearsal, with due notice taken of pacing and keeping the interest of the singers.

Between 9:00 and 3:00

The ideal time for a rehearsal with high school students is from an hour after school begins to an hour before school is over. Before 9:00 there are some of the problems encountered in the before-school rehearsal mentioned above, and in the final hour of the school day there are often interruptions for school functions. If you have a choice between early and late, however, take the late rehearsal.

The rehearsal of 50 or 55 minutes in a regular class period is an ideal time segment for high school students. If the rehearsal time is properly allocated to each item to be rehearsed or sight-read, there is no problem of loss of attention. Here is a general rule of thumb: *about 10 per cent of a rehearsal should be given to sight-reading and warm-up exercises after the first two or three weeks.* At the beginning of the fall term of school, about 20 per cent of the class (rehearsal) time should be allotted to warm-ups and sight-reading instruction. The reason for this emphasis is that on these solid foundations will be built the rest of the current year's choral music, as well as much of the choral program of future years.

49

Without proper instruction in the physical aspects of singing, and constant attention to the proper realization of this instruction, voices will not mature. Without sight-reading and ear-training instruction there will be constant leaning on the few instrumentalists who can already sight-read, or there will be a boring series of pecking out of parts by the accompanist.

The remainder of the class time should be a sequence of alternated styles of singing; that is, loud followed by soft, fast followed by slow, Latin followed by English, accompanied followed by unaccompanied. This may seem like an obvious procedure, but without knowing in advance which pieces you are going to work on, and particularly which *parts* of which pieces, you may have a solid half hour of slow, lugubrious, marvelous music which is gradually killing the spirit of the singers. Don't depend on the excellence of the music to carry a rehearsal. It is difficult to assess the greatness of a piece of music when you are bored and singing only one part.

If you have only one kind of music, you have probably chosen improperly because a program, no matter how brief and no matter how specialized the audience, should have contrast. Look to the writers of dance suites, sinfonias, and symphonies in the eighteenth century to see how time and tempo changes keep the interest of the listener through three, four, or a half dozen movements.

If all the works seem to begin in the same manner, pick out sections within the individual pieces which need rehearsal and work on these in a sequence which will give a sense of tension and then release to the rehearsal. The students may not know what is happening, and they probably would not care if they did know, but the psychological lift of changing styles is an essential in any rehearsal.

If the rehearsal is less than 40 minutes, you may have to shorten the sight-reading session slightly at the beginning of the semester. Ten minutes of sight-reading and 20 minutes of actual rehearsal, unless the sight-reading selections are chosen with extreme care, may wear on the nerves of high school students. However, as they become proficient in sight-reading they may ask for more and more pieces to read through.

50

This brings up another problem: facility in sight-reading but lack of enthusiasm for polishing. The solution is generally to demand that the singers memorize the piece and then take the music away from them as quickly as possible, usually before they have the music actually memorized. It is a strange truth that as sight-reading ability goes up, the ability to memorize goes down. The problem is to know when to take up the music. The general rule is: *before they want to give up the printed page, take it away from them.*

The Mini-Rehearsal

There have been scheduled rehearsals of only 20 or 25 minutes, which were generally the remaining half of a lunch hour or study period. Unless the voices have already been warmed up, a disproportionate part of the time is taken up by organizing and getting the voices in shape. The best solution is to get another, and longer, rehearsal period. That failing, you can only trim all of the elements of a rehearsal to a bare minimum and try to schedule another, and longer, rehearsal outside of schooltime.

The suggestions in the section concerned with before-school rehearsals will apply here. Combine warm-ups and sight-reading as much as possible, and pick a first number with limited ranges in the voices. Further, be extremely careful *not* to rehearse those sections the choir already knows. If there are five pages in a work and the main problems are on the last two pages, begin with those pages and ignore the easier pages until most of the problems have been worked out. *Never do a section the choir already knows just because it happens to come between two sections that need further work.* The only exception to this rule is when the known section is only a very few measures and the time required to stop and restart would be longer than continuing through the known section. Planning ahead is the only way to know which system to use.

These abbreviated rehearsals might be better used for part rehearsals, particularly if you have one or two student directors capable of taking a single section. This will be discussed further in Chapter 9.

Getting the Parents on Your Side

Parents are human, and like most human beings they want to take care of their own property, in this case the property being their own offspring. If you will take the time to type out an explanation of the rehearsal schedule, the good and bad points, and the alternatives to your rehearsal schedule, you will build an immediate band of backers. Misunderstandings come from a lack of information. Duplicate this letter and mail it to each parent. If you have a poor rehearsal schedule, it may come through in the tone of your letter, and this in turn may be brought up in PTA meetings or in conversations with School Board members, superintendents, or the principal. In your letter be sure to list the academic progress of the child (sight-reading, ear-training, proper pronunciation, fine literature), as well as the civic responsibilities (sunrise services, civic club programs) the child engages in. Parents want to know the whole scope of their child's development.

CHAPTER 5

Preparing for That
First Rehearsal

The first rehearsal of a group sets the tone for the entire year's work. If it consists of a well-ordered succession of enjoyable *and profitable* events, it has a decent chance to develop into a series of useful rehearsals. If one or more strategic elements happen to be left off or mismanaged in some way, you may find that a lot of future rehearsals will be uphill.

There are certain elements which need to be ready well before the first rehearsal. These include the Director's Folio, the cleaning off of old bulletin boards, and the readying of equipment listed in the first four chapters. Obviously, a minimum amount of music must be available for singing. Under no circumstances should the first meeting of a singing group be limited to a talk session on how great the coming season will be. The singers must experience a fine rehearsal in order to believe in the promise of upcoming successful rehearsals and programs.

Preparing the Choral Music

As the new music comes in, it will be necessary to mark each piece of music with some identifying stamp of either the school or the music department. Since first pages often get lost it is a good idea to stamp it twice, on the cover and on the first full page of music. No more stamping will be necessary, since the loss of a page of actual music automatically makes the remaining pages virtually useless.

It is common in many choral departments to assign a number to each singer or pair of singers. For each number there is a corresponding choral folder and a piece of choral music. The reasoning behind this procedure is to make the students responsible for the choral music. If a piece of music is lost, it is relatively easy to trace the missing number and simply ask the student to find the music or pay for a replacement copy. This places extra work on the director or the choral librarian, but it saves money in the long run. It is up to the individual director to decide if the saving in sheet music is worth the time spent. It takes a bit more time to pass out and take up the music which is numbered in this manner unless the pigeonhole method of distributing and collecting is used (see Chapter 1).

I prefer to emphasize to the students that I trust them, that someone will probably lose a piece of music, and that particular someone should be honest enough to tell me or the librarian and make the proper payment. If 40 or 50 copies of music are distributed, there will be one or two copies which will be lost and not paid for. I prefer this to the time-consuming nonmusical work of collecting 20- and 30-cent payments.

Sight-Reading Sheets or Octavos?

Whether dittoed, mimeographed, offset-printed, or purchased, the sight-reading material should be either in the folders (for octavo-sized sheets) or punched and ready for the students' notebooks. It is good for the singers to realize that sight-reading and basic theory is an integral part of the choral program. This goes for every chorus you direct, unless one chorus is drawn from another larger group which regularly gets sight-reading instruction and practice at another rehearsal. Sight-reading instruction will be covered more thoroughly in Chapter 6.

Chair Arrangements

As soon as the singers are chosen you should make a seating chart, no matter how basic. This can be as simple a process as blocking out a certain number of chairs for the sopranos, a certain number for the altos, and so forth, or it can be as elaborate as a particular chair assignment for each singer. The latter method presupposes a high degree of familiarity with each voice, its strengths and weaknesses.

Some of the traditional arrangements of choral sections have little to recommend them other than that they are familiar. The most common is to have the front rows assigned to the female voices and the back row or rows assigned to the male voices.

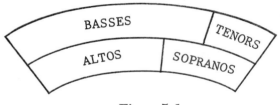

Figure 5–1

This has one fundamental weakness: the female voices are much louder than the male voices because the front row voices are much more "open" and unmuffled; whereas, the male voices are hedged in by heads, hair, and shoulders, all of which can absorb a lot of acoustical energy. In addition to this muffling of the male voices, there is the ever-present problem of fewer male voices, particularly tenors.

An alternative to this arrangement is the placing of the voices in vertical sections so that the front row of voices is more or less automatically balanced. My preference is shown in Figure 5–2.

Not only is the sound more balanced as a result of hearing a similar number of voices on each part, but a careful choice of front-row voices will give a cleaner sound. There is still another benefit, in that a voice which has occasional intonation problems

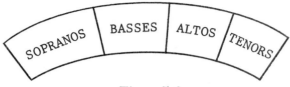

Figure 5–2

can be "buried" in the middle of a vertical section much more easily than in a two-row horizontal section. It is particularly helpful for the beginning singer to be surrounded with voices which are more accurate and confident.

Virtually all choirs, including most of the well-known professional choirs, occasionally have voices sing a part other than the assigned one. This is particularly true of the movement of voices between the alto and tenor lines in order to emphasize a particular vocal melody or give a distinctive vocal color. With the above seating plan it is quite simple for a few altos to fill out the high tenor notes, or on the other end of the scale, it is convenient for a few tenors to help the low altos in passages which need a contralto sound which is often missing in high school choirs.

The "scrambled" arrangement of voices for rehearsal will be explained in Chapter 6. It is enough to have a single seating chart with blocks of seats assigned to each of the sections. If the sections are further divided into first and second sections (Tenor I and II, Alto I and II, etc.), you may either have the seats so marked or you may choose to keep them in the basic four sections and work only on SATB music, which has no divided parts, for the first few rehearsals. This last plan is the safest and fastest idea, particularly when you are beginning rehearsals with a new chorus, or with a chorus which has a majority of voices which are new to you.

The Accompanist

The work and responsibilities of the accompanist will be covered more thoroughly in Chapter 10. On the first rehearsal, it is enough to say that he or she should have had the music long enough to play the parts as fast as the singers can learn them. Artistry is not the prime consideration at the first rehearsal.

The Basic Outline of the First Rehearsal

Unfortunately there is a certain amount of bookwork which is necessary at the first meeting of any school class, and this includes a chorus. A roll call may be quite rapidly given, but this is necessary and useful so new and old voices may meet each other. The election of officers should be put off until the natural leadership surfaces. Robe or uniform measuring can be put off until after hours. The rule is: *anything which can be put off until later, should be.*

The basic list of necessities is quite similar to the list for any rehearsal. Since 50 minutes seems to be about standard for high school classes, our outline of the first rehearsal will be based on that time span. You should include the following items:

1. Basic warm-up exercises.
2. Sight-reading material.
3. Three numbers which could be used for a program at a service club or PTA meeting.
4. Brief list of announcements, including a roll call of all members.

Various methods, techniques, and gimmicks for warming up a chorus are discussed at some length in Chapter 8. For our purposes, it should be emphasized that every rehearsal should include some type of warm-up exercise. These vocalises are much more than vehicles for clearing away frogs and clogged vocal machinery. They serve to make the ears more aware of intervals, to demonstrate the changes in quality and timbre when voices go from one part of the range to another, and they are voice-building devices. Only with regular and enthusiastic use of warm-up vocalises will the voices of your chorus develop the brilliance of a fine vocal ensemble. Only with simple vocalises can they concentrate on the mechanical aspects of voice production.

Sight-reading material can come from several basic sources but it must have two attributes: (1) it must be used regularly;

and (2) it must be comprehensive so that it teaches all intervallic and rhythmic combinations. It should be pointed out that this material should be more advanced than the sight-reading/warm-up material mentioned in Chapter 4. This sight-reading/warm-up series may be incorporated into the sight-reading course but the goals of sight-reading and warming up the voice are distinct. Only relatively easy and melodically obvious warm-up material should be used, so as not to distract the singers from the specific goal of training the voice (without, however, making them stupefyingly boring). The sight-reading material, on the other hand, should emphasize unusual intervals and intricate cross-rhythms. Chapter 6 explains some of the problems and gives some solutions in this area.

Self-preservation is the first law of the jungle and of school chorus directing. For this reason it is a good idea to choose the first three pieces for rehearsal, with the idea in the back of your head of using them on a program for some school or civic group meeting. *This does not mean all popular, or all sacred, or all trivial, or all anything.* There are far too many good, interesting, relatively easy concert pieces to delve into the banal for program selections. Also, remember that brevity has never been considered as a great hindrance to quality. Just as I prefer to see a two-minute demonstration of baton-twirling to a three-minute demonstration, so does the average listener at a public meeting (Kiwanis, School Board, Appreciation Dinners, and similar heterogeneous audiences) prefer a two-minute interesting number to a three-minute number. They have come to the meeting for other purposes.

Be sure that at least one of the numbers is a spritely, exciting type. It will not only help your program for a club, it will also help your rehearsal by providing a spark of excitement which might not be in the other two pieces. If this seems too obvious to mention, you should be aware of the possibility of programming only music which you prefer to hear. This type of preference-programming may not always include pieces with varying tempos, styles, and emotions.

It should not be your practice to rehearse only these three pieces until they are perfected. These are only to be emphasized. On the second rehearsal, you should substitute a new number for one of the original three. On the third rehearsal, read a new piece in place of one of the other two, and similarly for the fourth rehearsal. In this manner you will have a break from each piece, but you will still have worked on each piece three of the four first rehearsals. It takes planning, but by the end of the first week of rehearsals the original three pieces should be in excellent shape. Although this book is not primarily concerned with school politics, it should be pointed out that it has never been known to hurt a choral director to tell his principal during the second week of the school year that "I have three numbers ready if you need the choir for some program." This only comes about through proper planning of rehearsal time.

The last item which is necessary for the opening rehearsal is that ill-bred necessity, the announcements. Leaving off two or three important announcements and having to apologize at some subsequent rehearsal might cause a loss of confidence in a conductor's ability to manage. For this reason, as well as the saving of time, the announcements, roll calls, instructions about passing out and taking up music, future concerts, and similar necessary but nonmusical announcements should be listed in outline form. Since there will undoubtedly be some questions, it is best to leave at least ten minutes for these announcements. If there is time left, you can run through a piece one more time. Don't let the singers have the extra time for talking. This sets a precedent. Save that tidbit of released time until several rehearsals have gone well, then make it a five-minute reward for hard work.

It is helpful to keep the list of announcements in a file folder for reference next year. The announcements will vary slightly, but in general they stay the same. Your policy on tardiness and absenteeism should be consistent from year to year. Explanations concerning distribution and collection of music will probably remain the same. When a student argues that he did not know the rules, you can go to the files and show him what you read at the first rehearsal.

Progress and Enjoyment

The first rehearsal can prove to the students in your choir that choral music can be hard work which is highly enjoyable and mentally stimulating. This does not mean that every instant of every rehearsal will be a wildly exciting experience, but it does mean that every rehearsal can have several high points and that boredom will not be present .

That statement in the previous paragraph seems so obvious that it should not have to be made. However, as the age gap lengthens between you and your choir, and as your knowledge of choral literature grows, there will be a tendency to forget that what interests you as a musician may leave the students bored and distracted. Your excitement about certain pieces may carry the day, but on the first rehearsal it is best to be conservative in your choice of music. Most of your students will not be accomplished musicians, so just because a piece of music is an excellent example of a Renaissance motet or a Bach cantata excerpt, there is no guarantee that it will catch the students' interest on the first day. You will have an entire year to instruct the students in the finer elements of choral literature. They must be exposed to Renaissance motets, Baroque cantatas, as well as the choral works of Haydn, Brahms, and Barber, but common sense tells us that the first rehearsal should have more easily chewed material.

By and large, members of high school choirs are reasonably intelligent people. They usually have some inner drive to express something, and there is often a high correlation between their ability to sing and their mathematical or abstract analysis ability. They respond to explanations of why things work and why some objects have more artistic value than other similar objects. With this in mind, it is conceivable that the first week's rehearsal could be taken up completely with popular music. There are several current styles of arranging and writing popular music for a vocal ensemble. Using four highly contrasting styles of popular arrangements would do two things: (1) shows that you respect the area of music which affects them the most; and (2) shows that good and bad taste exists in all areas of music. There are some dreadfully old-fashioned arrangements from the 1940's and 1950's still selling regularly. You can show how styles change in choral arranging just as they change in clothing. It is my considered opinion that no high school student wants to be voluntarily ignorant about something which affects him very strongly. Popular music is really his domain. If you prove to him that he can exercise judgment within his own environment, you will have gained his confidence.

This is by no means a suggestion that the school year should begin with an investigation of popular music. It is only one of several avenues open to your choir. You might want to do three or four different types of choral pieces by Brahms, a sacred work, a secular work, and a folk song arrangement. Possibly three pieces from different musical eras which use the same text could make up a small program. The possibilities are almost endless for having variety and still maintaining unity. The main requirement is that the music have recognizable and explainable integrity.

Step-by-Step Through the First Rehearsal

With 50 minutes as our suggested average class length we can outline the rehearsal with some degree of exactness. If the students are coming from another class, they will probably just make it to the rehearsal room by the start of the period.

The first five minutes will be spent in getting the singers seated according to the chart. It may take slightly longer if you seat them in divided sections, Tenor I and II, Soprano I and II, and so forth. You may also take the time at the beginning of this first rehearsal to place the strongest musicians on the outside perimeter of the section. Don't worry about arranging the final concert formation for physical appearance. You won't want a boy 6'6" between two girls 5'1" during a concert, but for rehearsal it might be a good procedure.

The passing out of the music can take two forms: (1) the singers pick it up, or (2) someone passes it to them. If you prefer that the singers pick up the music, this could be the first item on your list. They should pick up the music before they are assigned a seat. If you pass out the music, this should be the first thing you do after the seating arrangements are completed. An alternate method is to place the music on the chairs before the rehearsal begins, or load the folders before the students arrive so that the time lost in passing out music is kept to a minimum.

Do not make the announcements at this time! Save them until the final ten minutes of the class meeting. The students have come to sing, so let them sing first, and then talk later.

The warm-up exercises should be relatively brief, possibly three or four minutes at the most. These should be concerned with getting the important body muscles working again after an appreciable layoff. The vocal quality will probably be shoddy, so work only enough to show some improvement but not enough to kill interest.

The sight-reading material should be brutally basic for this first rehearsal. Achievement is the main order of the day. The sight-reading might take five or six minutes, but not more than this, because it will eat into the time available for the actual singing. Due to the necessity of seating the singers and reading announcements, the rehearsal will be cut quite short.

Thus far from 15 to 20 minutes will have been spent in seating organization, passing out music, basic warm-ups, and sight-reading. The rest of the time until ten minutes before the end of the rehearsal should be spent in intensive, rapid-fire rehearsal of two or three numbers. Possibly only two pieces can be worked on, but each should have both a straight read-through and some work on detail. This will give the singers an idea of your general style of rehearsal. At times you will want to do several pieces straight through with only minimal correcting. At other times, you will work on details of one piece for 25 or 30 minutes at a stretch. The singers should know that both styles of rehearsing will be used. At the first rehearsal, do not just read through several pieces. There is an innate sloppiness about such reading which will give a false picture of the upcoming rehearsals.

Stop ten minutes before the end of the rehearsal, turn in your Director's Folio to the announcements page, and immediately begin reading. There is a certain professionalism which comes across when everything follows in a fast, logical order. Read positively, clearly, and loudly and answer questions briefly. If any time remains after the announcements you have made have been written down, *don't ask if there is anything you have left out.* Assume that you have everything under control. With the time remaining, you can go back to one of the pieces and work some more or read through one final piece you have not touched.

The emphasis throughout is on economy of motion and rapid-fire movement from one element of the rehearsal to the next. It is almost a law that any unoccupied time will be filled by conversation. Get the singers in the habit of listening while you are putting away one piece of music and getting out another. You, in turn, must develop the habit of talking while turning to the next piece of music. You must switch styles and tempos while flipping pages and preparing the singers for the next piece.

To be able to do this type of fast rehearsing, it is necessary to have a list of every item which will occur in the rehearsal. This can be placed on a small 3 × 5 card and clipped to your music stand, or laid in a prominent place near your music. Do not trust your memory. A very important piece simply might be forgotten under the pressure of rehearsing another work. The card will look something like Figure 5–3.

```
pass out music, get them seated
warm-up, teach intricate 5-step exercise
sight-read page 1, lines #1, #2, #3
read through My Country, 'Tis of Thee
      polish last page at tutti
      read through entirely
read God Bless America
      work men's section, page 7
      work entrances, p. 9
      entire work until 10 min. left
announcements
read America the Beautiful if time
```

Figure 5–3

This keeps the rehearsal on a steady course and allows you to go from one piece to another without thumbing through the music and pondering which piece to do.

CHAPTER 6

Conducting
Subsequent
Rehearsals
Effectively

It must be understood that there is no such thing as the *ultimate rehearsal*. There is only the *correct rehearsal for a given time*. Every day in a school year and every stage in the preparation of a program has special problems which must be solved before (and sometimes during) a specific rehearsal.

One of the main problems is combating sameness in a rehearsal. There must be warm-ups at the beginning, there should be some sight-reading to keep the mental agility at its peak, there may or may not be some announcements, and there are more or less familiar pieces which must be brought along at a predetermined pace so they are ready at a specific time. Within this framework of necessities, there must be some change to at least simulate freshness. Otherwise the predictability of the rehearsal period may become a drug to the attention of the singers. Interest span, depth of musical background, seriousness of artistic purpose, and chronological age vary from group to group and even between sections within a given chorus, and all of these items tend to keep techniques from being universally effective. For these reasons, we say the "ultimate rehearsal" is a figment of an imagination with limited practical choral conducting experience.

There are other areas which impinge on the rehearsal which may be adjusted or altered to give a freshness to the attitude. Every director has experienced the following: a visiting director or clinician has directed a work and in the process used the identical phrase you used at a specific passage, and suddenly the choir performed the passage the way you had originally wished. What actually happened was the suggestion came from a different sound source so the student singers instinctively feel that a brand new commandment has been handed down. Only the inflection was changed, but the message made a greater impression than when you did the speaking. For this reason, it is good to rephrase some of your favorite directing expressions. The singers become so accustomed to well-worn phrases that, like the sounds of a chiming clock, they soon learn to ignore them completely. It is necessary to use some rehearsal techniques which may be no better than the ones you are now using in order to give the impression of newness.

Thus, surprises will have to be planned carefully, and a constant regimen of self-evaluation started so that new (or simulated new) elements are brought into the rehearsal. In the process, there will usually be a fresh color to the choral sound. The seating arrangement can be altered, the entire rehearsal can be performed standing (if the singers are used to being seated), the rehearsal can be held in another room, you can use a baton (if you normally use your hands only), half of the group can listen to the other half being rehearsed, and several other variations are open to the inventive choral director (and there is no other kind of successful choral conductor on the high school level). Such areas as facial expressions, the use of English phrases (smooth like honey, slam the consonants), nonmusical imagery, or exaggerated gestures should be investigated.

Remember to use a larger conducting beat during early rehearsals than during the final rehearsals and the concert. The singers will be using peripheral vision for much of their visual contact with you. The better they know the music the smaller your beat can become, and this is particularly true of the left-hand gestures. Thus, in a given rehearsal the beat will vary in size according to how well-prepared the individual selections are. Wild gesturing is out of place on a memorized number and a small, almost indistinguishable beat is mostly useless with a complicated new work. The end result of uncontrolled conducting is visual fatigue for the singers. The audience has a tendency to become fatigued, also, when watching a human windmill at work.

The "Scrambled" Arrangement

There are various names for the arrangement which mixes voices from different sections: scrambled, integrated, quartet, intermix, and other variations on this theme. The idea is based on the fact that a singer must exercise better aural and oral control when singing while standing between two different musical parts, than when singing in a large section of his own voice part. Obviously it is much easier and faster to learn the music in sections, but after a certain point is reached in rehearsals it is a good practice to use the scrambled seating arrangement. This type of voice distribution tells you, the director, how well the individual singers know the music. It also tells the singers, themselves, how well or ill they know their individual voice lines.

The trouble spots become painfully apparent the first time this type of arrangement is used. The theory is simple: if the singers know their parts when separated, they will probably perform the piece properly when brought back together. Some choirs make a practice of performing in this integrated formation, although there are some valid arguments against the performance of certain musical styles in this manner.

While it is possible to carefully assign each student to a given seat in the scrambled arrangement, it is much less time consuming to instruct them to go to another part of the choir risers and make sure they are not standing next to anyone of their own voice part. This method is simple and fast, and the singers appreciate it since they can choose a friend to stand or sit beside rather than being assigned a specific position. In my own experience I have found no benefit to assigning definite places for scrambled singing, although I have occasionally moved a tall singer back or a short singer forward for sight reasons. Depending on how you look at it, this free-choice method of seating has either the advantage or disadvantage of allowing a different arrangement of voices each time you say "scramble." The advantages appear to outweigh the disadvantages in that, besides being fast, a new sound is presented to each of the singers each time they go into this arrangement. This forces them to listen to and adjust to different timbres, volumes, and vibratos which, in turn, forces them to make their own value judgments. To the conductor the sound is pretty much the same regardless of who stands where, unless a dominant solo voice happens to stand in the first row. In that case, it is best to "lose" that voice on the third or fourth row.

One admonition: *choose one term, whether "scramble," "integrate," "intermix," or whatever, and keep that term constant so the choir knows immediately what is expected of it.* Any time you can cut down on confusion you have saved rehearsal time.

There is a variation of this arrangement which might be used if a choir is extremely green, or if you have a particular style of music that has some polyphonic sections in it. This is the "modified scramble." Here only two sections mix into one, such as the sopranos and basses mixing while the altos and tenors form their own "mix." This particular arrangement has the advantage of pairing a high voice with a low voice. The variation of having the tenors mixing with the basses and the altos mixing with the sopranos is not as successful. The goal of this modified arrangement is to allow the singers to hear another part while singing their own, but not being confused with three other parts. This modified grouping is quite effective in concert, since you can still point to a general section while indicating an entrance for, say, the basses, and not have to confuse the tenors or altos. In addition, you can control the volume and articulation more readily since each section is spread over only half of the risers. Just form the word "bass" or "alto" or whatever with your lips and give the indication with your hands. If the individual sections sing much divisi music, the effectiveness of the modified arrangement is lost.

One of the great advantages in the scrambled seating arrangement is the improvement in pitch consciousness. It is quite easy for a voice, particularly a bass voice, to hang on the low side of the pitch and gradually pull the entire chorus down. Much more is demanded of the singers in this type of seating arrangement, but particularly in the realm of contemporary music and intricate arrangements of popular music.

As mentioned above, there are a few drawbacks to using the fully scrambled arrangement in presenting certain styles of choral music in concert. These would be mostly in the area of highly contrapuntal music, for instance most Renaissance motets and madrigals, many of the choruses in Handel's and Mendelssohn's choral works, as well as much twentieth century choral music. In music which emphasizes the horizontal line to a pronounced degree over the harmonic aspects, and where staggered entrances of parts cause different words to be sung at the same time, it is quite confusing to the audience to see a herd of singers all seemingly on different words. Such an arrangement usually does not give a clarity and definition of line which contrapuntal music requires. There are exceptions to this observation, but the danger is still present. In addition, it is difficult to control the dynamics and articulation of individual sections in the fully scrambled position. The modified scramble helps in this situation and also aids the audience in sorting out the individual voice parts visually. We often forget that a choral concert is a staged work as well as a sounded work.

In recordings, the modified scramble works quite well where one high and one low voice will be coming out of each speaker in a stereo recording. Usually, it is not necessary to separate the sections (that is, the soprano/bass group from the alto/tenor group) in order to get proper definition. Very seldom will you want a channel with only two of the voice lines and no hint of another part.

There is another benefit from having your group go into a scrambled formation during a rehearsal. It invariably livens them up and they start talking and laughing. It may be that you will use this device occasionally when a rehearsal is turning into a graveside scene. The lost 60 or 90 seconds on laughing and talking may allow you to salvage the remaining ten or 15 minutes for a decent rehearsal.

A cautionary note: *try this the first few times near the end of a rehearsal when only ten or 15 minutes remain.* The unusual effect may prove too exotic for the singers until some of the newness has worn off. Beginning too early in a rehearsal may lose an appreciable segment of time.

Dynamic Levels in Early Rehearsals

Don't enforce extremes of dynamic levels during the first few times through a piece. *Fortissimo* and *pianissimo* singing require energy best devoted to finding and singing the notes and rhythms. However, if you feel that the singers would benefit emotionally from hearing a passage at its eventual dynamic level, then work briefly on that passage but don't require such extremes all of the time. Too much work in certain areas may tend to make the concert anticlimactic.

First Use of the Risers

Do not wait until the morning of the program or concert to get the singers on the concert risers. There are a number of reasons for this warning: (1) the risers may be broken or at another school; (2) you may want a different standing order than the one you have in the rehearsal room; (3) the sound will be appreciably different when the rows are placed closer together and the short singers are singing into the hair and clothing of the row in front of them; (4) the new position will give the singers a different sound, which might throw them off their timing if they are somewhat inexperienced; (5) fatigue will be much more of a problem with the constant standing, unless they normally stand during the rehearsal; (6) the singers need to get over the physical excitement of being much closer together.

After ten or 12 rehearsals, set up the risers in the choral room (if space permits), or on the school stage, or even in the cafeteria. Use the last half of the rehearsal for getting arranged on the standing risers and allowing the singers to get a taste of the new sound. Use the last part of the rehearsal, because beginning the rehearsal with something as new as getting on the standing risers may throw the singers into an excitement which will ruin the rest of the rehearsal. Be sure to have the risers already set up so no rehearsal time is lost in purely mechanical areas. It will take at least ten minutes to get the students on the risers and properly arranged. If time permits, it is helpful to move the rows around so each singer has a chance to sing on both the front and back rows.

There are nonmusical elements which enter into concert-riser placement. Excessively fat or thin girls should be placed back of the front row to minimize their distracting silhouettes. I had one soprano who suffered with a severe vertigo problem and she could not stand on even the first row of the risers. This meant placing her on the floor, but she was tall, so the singers in back of her also had to be relatively tall. These problems should be isolated and taken care of well in advance of concert day.

If it appears that excitement is going to carry the day and your rehearsal is being wasted, use the time to work on nonmusical items. Show the students how to hold the music correctly when they are singing from scores. Try different lighting situations so they will not be blinded by the full light hitting them during a concert. Have them practice walking on and off the risers until they can do it without being self-conscious and without watching every step they take. If you use seated risers, have them practice rising and sitting without looking around to be sure there is a chair there (have them back up against the chair so their legs tell them where the chair is).

Half Listening, Half Performing

One point often overlooked in rehearsals is the fact that singers can learn music even when they are not singing. If a choral singer almost knows a part, he or she can often pick up valuable information from listening to another group perform the piece. For this reason it is a useful technique to divide your choir into two equal parts, balancing the sections as well as possible (equal numbers of Bass I and II and Alto I and II in each group). Place the choirs on opposite sides of the rehearsal hall and begin the rehearsal.

There are various ways in which this split-chorus rehearsal can be run. You may want to rehearse an entire section with first one group, then the other. This alternating of choirs helps each to hear and perform. Another method keeps the students' attention glued tightly to the music. This occurs when you inform both

71

groups that you will alternate between the groups, but not at a particularly logical place in the music. Thus, for example, the first group might sing "My Country, 'tis . . . ," the second group would get the signal to continue ". . . of thee, sweet land of . . . ," the signal would flash again and the first group would finish ". . . liberty, of thee I sing." In practical application, the phrases would be much longer for each group. The reason for this switching between groups at awkward places is to keep the full attention of each singer in the group which happens to be listening. This cuts down on the horseplay and the signalling to friends which might occur if one group were left alone for an appreciable period of time.

Moving to Another Room

All ears, including a conductor's, tend to become somewhat insensitive to certain distortions or mistakes over a period of time. These blind spots can be partially eliminated by moving the rehearsal to another room, or sometimes even to another part of the same room. Each room has its own particular acoustical characteristics, which means only that certain timbres are reinforced and others deadened or distorted. If another room of appreciable size is available, just post a note on the rehearsal room door that says the current rehearsal is being held in the band room, or the cafeteria, or the gymnasium, or on the stage, or in the boiler room. Have the risers or chairs already in place so that no time is lost in trying to find the best arrangement. Choose a room, if possible, which has extreme acoustic characteristics in comparison to the rehearsal room. Procure an all-concrete room where the sound rings and echoes, then find one which is as dead as possible. Singing on a stage with the curtains closed is about as dead as you can find, particularly if the loft is relatively high and cluttered with old scenery and drapes.

Sometimes just moving the chairs forward a few feet will produce a new sound. While giving a concert with a high school chamber choir of 12 voices, I once found a totally confusing sound coming back to the singers. It was a total "wipeout." Nothing was in tune and their confidence was going fast. We found some drapes behind us so we partially opened the drapes, and at the same time, pulled the portable stage forward about 2 feet. The change in sound was fantastic. The chords fell into place, the soloists could be heard by the entire group, and of great importance, their confidence returned. If your choir normally sings toward a flat wall, give the risers a 45-degree turn so it is singing toward a corner. If the room is oblong, and the risers or chairs are moveable, turn 90 degrees and move back and forth to get another sound.

The purpose of all of this moving around (and you won't need to do such moving more than twice a month) is to get both you and the singers out of bad habits of hearing. Everyone gets used to certain sounds, and whether right or wrong, we begin ignoring these sounds. Rehearsing in a different room puts the familiar sounds in a different perspective.

Remember, there probably will not be a piano in the room you use for this moved rehearsal. Use music which does not require major pianistic support. Use music which is virtually ready for concert presentation, because the emphasis in such rehearsals is on rehearing and rethinking about music which has fallen into a groove. Work on pronunciation, intonation, entrances and cutoffs, crescendos and diminuendos. In other words, everything but the notes themselves. Work on those in the regular rehearsal room.

Beginning the Rehearsal

The problem which eats up rehearsal time at a fantastic rate is the one of habitually starting late. Make it a practice to start when the bell rings, even if you only have four singers. It may appear that you have only lost a small amount of time during the warm-up, but if you are a conscientious director you will always have a solid warm-up and sight-reading session, so in actuality you are chopping this lost time off the end of the rehearsal. This is your prime rehearsal time, when your singers are in the best voice and going strong. The sin of starting late is compounded when the rehearsal is quite short, possibly only 25 or 30 minutes. We have already stated that a 25-minute rehearsal is actually only 18 or 19 minutes in length. Habitually losing two or three minutes in late starts cuts that down to only 15 or 16 minutes of rehearsing.

Sight-Reading Techniques

There are several fine sight-reading courses available which will work well on the high school level. However, some of them are based on a one-semester or two-semester course of study where a considerable part of the class time is given to sight-reading and ear-training. It is my belief that the most profound need for the high school chorister is for a series of brief excerpts which will illustrate the three main areas of vocal music: rhythm, interval relationships, and diatonic melody. Since you, the director, know the level of your singers better than anyone else, it is only logical that you should be the one to prepare the sight-reading material. Although this sounds at first like a large undertaking, it actually is not. Only a few hours of work will be required to prepare enough material for an entire semester of sight-reading instruction.

This suggestion is based on the fact that you do not need material for extensive practice, you only need to illustrate the problems of sight-reading. The choral material you will be performing will constitute the extension of the basic sight-reading course. Since you will be trying to teach each item (rhythm, interval, diatonic melody), you will need to write some simple exercises which use each interval or rhythmic combination. There is no need for them to have a whole page of exercises which work on the interval Middle C to the G above. One or two lines of exercises will illustrate what is necessary to their understanding. It is best to make each page illustrate: (1) a particular interval or pair of intervals, or (2) a particular area of the keyboard.

Figure 6–1 shows some exercises which work on hearing the

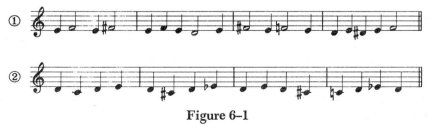

Figure 6–1

74

difference between a major and a minor second. The exercises make no musical sense taken by themselves; they are merely exercises.

Figure 6–2 works primarily on major and minor thirds, although there is obviously an occasional major or minor second thrown in to give some musical credence to the vocal line.

Figure 6–2

As the number of intervals increases, there will be a gradual slowing of the rate of introduction of new intervals so the singers can work on the intervals in combination. Figure 6–3 is an example of the combining of major and minor seconds with major and minor thirds to give an almost atonal series of notes.

Figure 6–3

These pieces have been used with high school students of varying musical backgrounds, and even with one junior high school class. It is obvious that two elements must be present: (1) the singers must understand the treble and bass clefs; and (2) the director must understand the necessity of being able to sight-read *and he must be enthusiastic about it*. Some directors are skeptical about the value of teaching an extensive sight-reading course until they experience the boost a choir gets from learning music more rapidly than before the sight-reading training began. The five or ten minutes taken in each rehearsal for the first ten or 12 weeks will be more than made up in time saved at piano plunking.

The rhythmic training is along the same lines, with simple combinations at the beginning, such as Figure 6–4,

Figure 6–4

progressing to,

Figure 6–5

and finally to such works as these complicated rhythms sung as a canon:

Figure 6–6

The easiest part of sight-reading instruction is that of simple diatonic melodies. Teach these with some type of solfege syllables or numbers so the singers will get a feeling for certain areas and "notches" in the diatonic scale. Constantly calling attention to the tonic and dominant in rehearsal will mean nothing to them until they understand that *do* or *one* remains the same throughout a tonic piece. This building of tonal memory for the diatonic scale, and particularly of the tonic and dominant, is the very heart of proper intonation in choral singing. Students learn very rapidly to remember where the tonic and dominant are located, whether you call them *do* and *sol* or *one* and *five*. They also can learn to tune to a remembered tone of a measure or two before. This is not an attempt to train the students to have perfect pitch. Rather it is a practical and workable attempt to train singers to hear notes before they sing them.

This diatonic melodic training can be quite boring, unless you keep it interesting and at least modestly exciting. Exciting does not mean wild, it merely means something which grabs the sing-

76

ers' attention and which is worthwhile. The addition of numbers or syllables to the singing of the melodies helps to solidify the individual notes of the diatonic scale more readily than merely singing a neutral vowel. It also helps a section stay together when singing a round or canon. Figure 6–7 shows an early diatonic melody exercise.

Figure 6–7

Later these can be more complicated rhythmically, but not until the exact steps of the diatonic scale are firmly established in the singers' ears.

Figure 6–8

Finally, there can be some slight chromatic alteration of notes as long as the basic feeling of a diatonic melody remains. Upper and lower neighboring tones, chromatic passing tones, altered tones in minor, and other basic musical changes can be used.

Figure 6–9

These exercises can be placed on ten-staff or 12-staff Spirit Duplicator Stencils and run off for less than 50 cents per 100. They should be punched for three-ring notebooks and become part of the students' regular musical equipment which is brought to each rehearsal. The best procedure is to have a 12-staff page devoted to the following: four lines of interval drill, two lines of rhythm drill, and six lines for diatonic melody. As the singers progress, it may become apparent that one area, for instance rhythm, needs more work and explanation. You simply have four lines of rhythm exercises and only four lines of diatonic melody.

If your group is an average group, it will learn the number system or sol-fa system fairly quickly. There will be some exceptions, but enough of them will understand it so that the group can get through fairly intricate material on the first attempt. To keep the singers' interest, to sharpen their aural discrimination, and most particularly to prepare them for dissonant, nonpredictable contemporary music, have them sing all exercises as rounds, entering by sections on successive measures. Some melodies which are built around only the tonic and dominant chords may sound quite bland, and you may even wish to use some little-known canons or rounds for melodic practice. On the other hand, some of the melodies should be constructed so that harsh clashes occur. This will require the singers to hold their own notes against the harmonic pull of notes by other sections.

The following looks harmless enough,

Figure 6–10. *Diatonic melody.*

but the following sounds are the results of this melody being sung as a round:

Figure 6–11. *Melody as a round, with piano reduction.*

Students cannot accidentally sing this type of material. They must learn the technique in rehearsal.

I have found that when singing these melodies as a round it is easier to alternate men/women/men/women. Thus, the procedure is to read through with everyone, then read it as a round consecutively with sopranos, tenors, altos, and basses, each part coming in on the beginning of each successive measure. The next time reverse the order to bass, alto, tenor, and soprano. It is also possible to enter after three beats in 4/4 or after three beats in 3/4 to give unusual rhythmic stresses. This last technique can be used with any melody, familiar or not, to unlimber ears for more dissonant choral works.

It is only natural to be concerned at the student's reactions to such dissonant and unusual material as that illustrated in the previous passages. No amount of encouragement from this book can equal the effect of trying two or three pages and seeing the immediate improvement in music reading and performance. A rehearsal is a time devoted to preparing singers for presenting choral music. Anything which improves the quality of the choral presentation should become a basic part of the rehearsal schedule.

The time devoted to sight-reading training should vary from five to ten minutes for each rehearsal, with the obvious limitations of a very short rehearsal or a concert only two or three days away. However, don't just prepare four or five of these sheets, work on them for a couple of weeks and then try to head into a solid diet of difficult choral music. Sight-reading should be a consistent part of each rehearsal for the entire first semester, and ideally even longer. There is almost no end to the ability of high school students to learn intricate sight-reading skills. The lack is usually found in the director's enthusiasm.

Interval training can be facilitated by two devices, both of which have worked well with high school students. For diatonic intervals hold up one hand with the fingers indicating the numbers from one to five, these representing the first five degrees of the major or minor scale. When they can move back and forth from any number in either scale to any other number, divide the chorus in half with one half following one hand and the other half following the other hand. It takes a bit of coordination and experience, but you can get some fine ear-training out of the first five degrees of a scale. Then, try one hand in major and one in minor. Afterwards, have one group in one key and the other in a key a major third away.

For interval training with atonal melodies or isolated intervals, place 12 circles or squares on the chalkboard in a vertical line. These stand for the 12 semi-tones in the chromatic scale. Move back and forth from one to the other, or in every possible combination, starting from the bottom or from the top note. An incidental benefit will be the sharpening of the conductor's ear.

See Appendix I for sample sight-reading sheets.

When to Close the Octavos

There comes a time in all series of rehearsals when the singers see but they do not observe, to use Sherlock Holmes' phrase. The notes are almost completely assimilated, the words are under control, and the singers have a general idea about the dynamics. Just before your choir reaches this stage, have them begin performing from memory. Even if you intend to use music during the concert, have them sing as much as possible from memory. To do this, have the accompanist play very softly so the musical continuity is not lost, while you mouth the words to the section which has trouble with the text. This is one of the best means of proving to the singers that they actually know much more of the music than they thought possible.

Now is the time to instruct the singers in the technique of holding music during a concert It may seem contradictory that learning to hold the music open and singing from memory should be discussed in the same section, but the two problems are related. Most of the music must be memorized, even when singing with open scores. The printed music is only for reference and reminding, not for constant reading. The singers should have the general outline and the text for each phrase solidly in mind. When the choir sings, the music should be held approximately 15 inches from the face and about 45 degrees below horizontal. One hand holds the music or folder at the fold; the other hand does all of the page turning. The head remains facing straight forward, with only the eyes moving when reading the music. This keeps the voice from going directly into the book.

There is a problem, of course, when there are too many singers for the available space on the risers. A compromise with music only on the first and third rows might be necessary, with rows two and four looking over shoulders.

As much as possible get the singers into the habit of holding the music in this position during rehearsal. It may feel awkward or even affected at first. Only constant use will make it more comfortable. As with most instructions, the singers will gradually fall into old habits of constantly looking at the music with the head bowed and the eyes glazed. When this happens your only recourse short of physical aggression is to have the singers fold the music and go through the section by memory.

Memorizing Outside of the Rehearsal

Rehearsal time is too valuable to use for memory-repetition. If you decide to memorize a piece, plot the rehearsal sequence so the notes are learned before the memorizing is finished. Do not wait until one section is memorized before polishing another. The best way to get the memorizing out of your hair is to divide the choir into several small groups of about eight voices, assign a leader to each group, and require them to memorize the music outside of class. It is best not to expect them to work on notes by themselves because there is a tendency to just memorize whatever comes handiest. Be sure the entire group can go through the piece without faltering, then let them memorize it. After it is memorized, you can do the final polishing. A word of caution: *you will need a club of some kind to hold over the heads of certain students.* Unfortunately, some high school students are not mature enough to see the value in individual memorization, so you can exclude them from participating in the concert, keep them from making the trip with the rest of the choir on away contests, or some such penalty if they do not memorize the required pieces. The only way you can check on the status of their memorizing is by listening to each octet individually. You may wish to hear them by quartets. Don't assume that because the entire group can get through the work without the music that everyone has it memorized. Memorizing by sections doesn't work as well because the singers won't have the sound of the entire work in their ears.

How Much Emotion?

Should you try to keep the emotional level of each piece at the highest peak possible, or should it vary with each rehearsal? Although it will certainly vary with each piece and each choir, it is generally not a good idea to try to keep a piece at a very high plateau of excitement throughout its rehearsal period. There are works which can sustain this excitement, but there is a considerably larger body of works which wear out relatively quickly. Popular music is almost universally within this category. The early excitement is sustained by the familiarity of the melody and text. When these are sung and resung by bits and pieces in rehearsal, the excitement quickly pales.

You will feel a gradual lessening of excitement or emotion with almost any work. The telltale signs are the making of mistakes where there were none before and the drooping of pitch. It may be best to leave the number alone for a few rehearsals. Then, when you take it up again, rehearse with all the fire and enthusiasm you have. Show the singers that it is not the music but the performers' attitude toward the music which makes it less exciting.

If you try to keep the emotional level high during the rehearsal, there may be nothing left for the singers at the concert. It takes a bit of courage, but on the last rehearsal before a program or concert work on short sections of the music rather than on entire works. The singers will want to do complete works straight through from the beginning, mostly because this will give them a certain sense of security in performing what is well known. Your problem is to keep their emotions bottled up at the dress rehearsal or the warm-up period before a concert so the concert will be the release of the excitement, not the rehearsal period. This certainly does not preclude many exciting moments during the rehearsal of any number, but the excitement should taper down just before a concert is scheduled.

Most rehearsals should finish strong. This can mean the singing of either a loud or a soft piece, but it should have a strong emotion. Just tapering off with working on tuning one or two chords, or letting the altos sing a phrase five times does not leave the singers with a feeling of having completed anything. Let them leave having sung a complete piece or at least a complete section.

The Announcements

The question of selecting the right time to make the necessary announcements cannot be answered exactly for all situations. Generally speaking, they should not be the first or the last detail of a rehearsal. The first part should be singing or warming up. The last event should be the singing of some emotional or exciting work. The best place I have found is right after the sight-reading. The singers are about as mentally alert as they will become, so they should retain most of what you tell them.

Varying the Styles of Music

No rehearsal should consist of only one style of music. Even within the confines of an extended work by one composer there will be contrasting styles available for rehearsing—homophonic and polyphonic, fast and slow, loud and soft. Performing one style for 25 or 30 minutes dulls the senses, so that a law of diminishing choral returns presents itself. Even going to a less exciting section can be a goad to the singers to get more work accomplished.

There may come a time when you need to get one section ready for a concert which is only a day or two away. Then you have to gimmick the work so that it appears different and more interesting while still getting the rehearsing accomplished. One method is to increase or decrease the speed grotesquely. This throws the entire piece into a different perspective. What is normally taken at $\quarternote = 84$ is a brand new set of notes at $\quarternote = 48$.

Conversely, a Bach chorale taken at double the regular speed forces a concentration on different aspects of the music.

It is also possible to sing the piece staccato or with each note over an eighth note sung as an eighth. The singers must count more accurately as well as sing without swooping into notes. A section which is loud may be sung pianissimo, but for some reason a soft passage sung loudly is not as effective. It usually sounds merely out of taste. Raising and lowering the pitch is not as effective as other alterations, since in either case two sections are singing either too high or too low for decent tone control or production.

Baton or Hands?

This is strictly a matter of personal preference in concert, but during rehearsal there is much to be gained by going back and forth from directing with the hands to directing with a baton. Some of this benefit accrues to the director in the form of improving his conducting technique, but most of the benefit is in the attention given the conductor by the singers.

For some reason, there has been a stigma attached to directing a chorus with a baton. This is totally unfounded. It is no more "wrong" to direct a chorus with a baton than it is "wrong" to direct an orchestra with hands only. Certain effects are often more easily obtained with one or the other, and this is the fundamental reason for conducting a work first one way, then the other. Don't use one of the long buggy-whip batons. Get a shorter choral baton. And don't be afraid to pick up or drop the baton in the middle of a phrase if the change will improve the rehearsal.

Plotting the Rehearsal

Each rehearsal must be plotted with regard to two basic needs: (1) the requirements of the upcoming concert, and (2) the psychological needs of the singers. The first of these should be the most important consideration. Or rather, it should be the first consideration. When these concert requirements have been determined, they can then be placed in an order according to the best psychological pattern for a strong rehearsal. A rehearsal can be satisfying to a singer and still be a total loss as far as ground gained is concerned. Conversely, a lot of material can be learned, but the singers might be left with a foul taste for both the rehearsal and the music.

Some pieces rehearse easily as a unit, some rehearse best in fits and starts. If a piece is made up of several small sections, there is no law that requires a known section be sung just because it comes before or after a section which is still in a rough condition. Find the areas which are giving your singers the roughest time and work on them, then move backward and take these rough areas in the context of the entire section. This may seem to be an obvious procedure, but some conductors occasionally fall into the habit of saying "take it from the top" or "let's do it again" without adding up the time spent in wearing out the music which is already learned. Of course, in those places where it would take longer to find the notes than to start again, this admonition does not apply.

In this type of rehearsal which emphasizes the cleaning up of small areas, it is often useful to "rehearse in reverse"; that is, start with the last problem area, work it out, move back to the next to last problem, work that out, continue to the end of the piece, and so forth. Each time a problem is solved, continue on to the end of the work. This has the tremendous benefit of giving the singers added confidence in the final pages of the work. Moving toward an area that is well known is considerably more enjoyable than moving toward a series of rocky shoals.

This rehearsing in reverse is also a good procedure to use in music which is in good shape but not quite memorized. The first pages are usually the first ones committed to memory. Taking the last section, then the last two sections, then the last three, etc., gives the singers practice on parts which they probably know the least well.

Certain guides should help in determining what areas need the most work:

- Works which are learned but not fully memorized.
- Works which have ragged sections among good sections.
- Works where dynamics need the most attention.
- Works with pronunciation problems.
- Works which need attention to entrances and cutoffs.

This spans the entire gamut of choral singing. Your problem as director is to give some form of precedence to each item as it appears on your list. Should you try to memorize even when there are a handful of chords which are still hazy? Can you work on dynamics when some notes are still not under control? Which must come first in a certain section, exact rhythm or exact pronunciation? These questions will appear before each rehearsal and you will need to answer them before you can begin any rehearsal. It is generally best to work some on each area listed above, rather than go through a complete rehearsal concentrating only on pronunciation or working only on entrances and cutoffs.

When the list of the greatest and most pressing needs is completed, edit it down to a size that will fit your rehearsal period, remembering the other elements which must be in all rehearsals. From this edited list select a good closer, some piece which is exciting and can be successfully rehearsed with a minimum amount of work. The reason for this is to provide a satisfying close to the rehearsal for the singers. It may be best to work backward in organizing the rehearsal. Choose the best piece to close with, then choose a contrasting problem to go just before the closing piece, then another problem just before that, and so forth until you get back to the warm-ups and sight-reading at the beginning of the rehearsal.

Place this material on a 3×5 card. This card should be clipped to your music stand or laid in a prominent and easily seen place for constant reference during the rehearsal. Place approximate times next to the individual items if you find it helpful. Don't be afraid to eliminate a piece chosen for rehearsal if another work is going extremely well, but keep the end of the period in mind. Your card should look something like Figure 6–12.

Anything less than this in the way of organization will allow some important spots to go by unnoticed until the last rehearsal, at which point some directors have been known to panic. This is generally followed by panic on the part of the singers.

Besides being psychologically satisfying to the singers, thoughtful preplanning and a sense of organization are also helpful in getting the director "up" for the rehearsal. All directors want a useful and valuable rehearsal, and the prospects of getting some good work accomplished is one of the best pep rallies for the director. Few things kill the rehearsal as much as seeing the di-

```
warm-up, work tenor head voice
sight-read p. 3, lines #5 & #6
read through My Country 'Tis of Thee
work detail on America the Beautiful
     p. 3, women's entrance
     p. 5, solo part with chorus
     p. 9, tune chords at tutti
     sing entire work slow, then fast
work God Bless America in reverse
sing climax of Star Spangled Banner
```

Figure 6–12

rector leafing through the music pondering which piece needs work. Few things impress the students as much as a rapid movement from one piece to another, with precise comments about where to work and why to work that particular place.

CHAPTER 7

Developing Proper
Choral Tone and
Style in the
Rehearsal

One chapter could not hope to cover the entire area of either choral tone *or* style in choral singing. However, there are certain fundamental concepts which need to be examined because of their relationship to rehearsal techniques. Without these concepts clearly in mind during the preparation of a choral work in rehearsals, there might be a tendency to develop one basic choral sound or timbre—and then that sound would be used for all music of all periods. Or worse, any convenient choral tone might be used for any choral work of any type. It takes only a few weeks of rehearsing to realize that some types of choral music respond more quickly to specific choral timbres than to others. Trying to force the wrong style of sound on a piece of music might waste rehearsal time, as well as keep the work from getting the proper interpretation.

Directing the Music or the Composer?

It is always a revelation to a director to rehearse a complete concert of the music of one composer. Unless there is a deliberate attempt to perform only one type of music, the concert will usually turn up several compositional techniques, each of which may require a different type of choral sound. Also, each of these compositional techniques will require a different rehearsal technique. Brahms is the composer who comes to mind most readily. There is a vast difference in the timbre requirements between the *German Requiem* and the folk song arrangements. In between are the shorter choral works (*Nänie, Schicksalslied, Gesang der Parzen,* and others) and the works for an ensemble of solo voices (*Liebeslieder Walzer* and other sets of works). It would be unthinkable to have the same vocal color for each of these pieces, or even the same tone color for all of the *Liebeslieder* waltzes for that matter. Each piece of music, no matter how small, sets up its own requirements for interpretation, and these are firmly embedded within the music.

It is quite common to hear musicians speak of a "Mozart sound" or a "Palestrina sound" or a "Brahms sound," particularly among choral musicians. This generally means that there are certain types of vocal sounds which work best with these widely separated styles of composition. It is relatively widely understood that a Brahms motet will have a different sound than a Palestrina motet. The problem is to understand why this should be so and how the different qualities should be obtained during rehearsal.

With a tiny handful of exceptions, most composers wrote in several different styles—sometimes homophonic, sometimes polyphonic, sometimes an accompanied melody. For this reason, you should never conduct a piece in a specific manner just because it was written by a given composer. Your rehearsal schedule will vary from piece to piece, even within individual sections of an extended work. It has been emphasized in previous chapters that there is no ideal rehearsal schedule other than the one which utilizes every moment most fully. There are different techniques for rehearsing a large chorus and a small chamber ensemble, for homophonic and polyphonic works, and for male chorus, female chorus, and mixed chorus works. Generally speaking, if the style is right, the rehearsing will be easier.

There is a basic pitfall in describing sounds with words: *all words do not mean the same thing to all people.* This makes all verbal and written communication *about sound* dangerous and suspect, including this one. Because of the various meanings of certain common words such as "soft," "heavy," or "bright," word descriptions occasionally give an improper meaning. Nevertheless, it is often necessary to describe sounds to a choir, using images and descriptions from nonmusical sources. Merely to describe a sound as "Mozartean" or "Wagnerian" to an amateur choir is to waste breath and rehearsal time. There must first be the concept of a correct sound found through experiment or trial and error, and then some word or phrase must be found which triggers the right sound from the choir. The word or phrase will differ from choir to choir and from one part of the country to another.

How Was It Originally Performed?

Since the rehearsal schedule is determined by what you hope to obtain from the choir, it is necessary to determine accurately in your mind what the ideal performance would be, keeping in mind that the ideal performance is determined by the music itself, not by what has previously been done with or to the music. This makes it necessary to understand when and why the music was first written. Some music was never meant to be performed on a concert stage. This includes virtually all of the music with a sacred text written before about 1750. The music was designed to fill a particular notch in a church service, and as such it could be much less spectacular and still be a successful work. On the other hand, many works from this period were meant for a relatively musically sophisticated audience which could understand subtleties and nuances not felt by modern audiences. Directors who choose to perform this music in a concert-with-audience situation must walk the fine line between being dull but authentic (some of the original performances must have been roaring horrors by modern standards) and hyperemotional but stylistically wrong. Obviously, a special concert sung before a group of trained musicians would not have the limitations of a concert for a high school assembly or even a Spring Concert attended by a general audience.

The classic example of this problem is in the motets of the late Renaissance (Palestrina, Marenzio, Hassler, Praetorius, and others). Originally these motets were performed by either a solo ensemble or a small choir which usually had boys' voices on the soprano line and men singing counter-tenor (a type of trained falsetto) on the alto line. In addition, instruments were often used to double the vocal lines or even to take the lines alone if the specific voices were not available. We can readily see that the sound of a 16-voice choir of Boys/Falsettoists/Tenors/Basses would differ radically from the sound of 60 high school boys and girls. The most noticeable effect would be in the clarity of line available to the original choir of male voices. Each line would have a different tone quality and would stand out in stark relief. On the other hand, a high school choir usually has little differentiation between altos and sopranos except that one sings lower than the other. One director characterized the sound as that of "high mezzo-sopranos and low mezzo-sopranos." This problem is further complicated by the occasional addition of altos to the tenor line to beef up the volume or to relieve the tenors of unseemly high notes. Finally, the voices often cross, particularly between the altos and tenors, or if there are two soprano parts. It is an absolute stylistic necessity that these parts remain distinct entities and do not blend into a pseudo-homophonic work.

The rehearsal must be organized so that time is spent explaining the problems to the singers. They must understand that their blending must be within sections and not between sections in this older music. This will necessitate some time with individual section rehearsal (see Chapter 9). It takes some experimenting with a section to get the proper sound because the singers must try several different tongue and lip positions.

It is at this point that our problems of style usually appear. In an effort to make the music "pretty," these early works are often given abrupt dynamic and tempo changes as well as long crescendos, decrescendos, and ritardandos. These are superimposed on the austere music to make it more palatable to the audience. Since this book is not concerned primarily with musical ethics, we will not attempt to say whether this is permissible or should be abolished. However, adding this type of interpretation to the music requires considerably more rehearsal time than merely singing the music with altered tone quality. The latter method may not be as immediately appealing to the average audience unless it is given some hints about listening procedures.

The rehearsal for this more romantic approach to interpretation requires individual phrasing of the vocal line to a more extensive degree than with merely adjusted tone quality. In completely or almost-completely polyphonic music, the crescendos and diminuendos will generally follow the rise and fall of the melodic line. This means they will not fall at the same time in the individual voices. When the tone quality is more homogeneous, as in the average high school choir (where the vocal lines are less individualistic), these rises and falls of the melody are less distinguishable and must be made more pronounced with volume changes. These take rehearsal time.

It also takes time to obtain the equivalent of the older vocal timbres. The basses and tenors are not a problem since they should sing with a normal production and quality, the differences in range taking care of the separating of the lines by the listeners' ears. It is best not to add altos to the tenor line, unless the altos can match the tone quality of tenors in the upper part of the tenor range. The altos would be singing in their lower or midrange and would be much more mellow and less intense. This would dilute the effect of the tenors' high notes. On the other hand, the alto line must have its own brand of intensity. Imitation may be the only effective way of teaching altos to produce a counter-tenor sound. Have the tenors sing a phrase in falsetto. This will require some rehearsal time since the tenors should sing with musicality and proper intonation. Then have the altos attempt to match this sound. The older the alto section the more difficulty the individual voices will experience, since the mature alto sound is much heavier and "darker" (if this is a good term).

Many high school singers do not know the sound of a well-trained boy choir so they will have trouble duplicating the sound at first. Ask them to sing a pure, straight tone with as much brilliance as possible, but not very loud. The resulting tone should be almost instrumental in character, which is the proper direction to go. The idea is to get a tone which is mildly nonhuman, an ethereal sound which does not partake of human emotionalism. This does not mean it should be entirely nonemotional, but rather that the music should have a staid, introspective quality about it which is above mere humanity.

Using these altered tone qualities also enables the singers to hear each individual section more clearly, since each voice stands out in sharp relief in a single chord as well as in polyphonic passages. This improves intonation which in turn saves rehearsal time. Any rehearsal technique which makes mistakes more obvious to the singers will in the long haul save time.

What has been mentioned about polyphonic music of the late Renaissance can be applied to polyphonic music of any period up to our current year. When the dominant emphasis is on individual lines, there is a necessity for the director to make sure that each line can be heard and understood. Most assuredly this does not mean using a Medieval or Renaissance tone quality on a piece by a contemporary composer. It does mean, however, that vocal lines which are rich and full are sometimes less obvious in a web of polyphonic sound than a "thin, bright" tone. This is illustrated most effectively by some recent recordings of Handel's *Messiah*. The traditional method of using a large orchestra of about 100 players with a chorus of 200 or more usually gives a thick, heavy-footed feeling to the fast, polyphonic choruses. The newer recordings and performances have used choruses of from 35 to 40, with orchestras numbering in the 30's. It is much easier for eight or ten sopranos to sing a sparkling and rhythmically alive vocal line than 50 or 100 sopranos. This does not mean 100 sopranos cannot be accurate; it only means that more rehearsal time will be required to clean up attacks and releases and to balance the sections.

A large chorus is additionally handicapped by having a greater distance between the outside edges of the risers. There is a time lag in the sound reaching the opposite side of the choir, which in turn tends to blur sharp rhythms, particularly ♪. ♪ in Handelian choruses. This can be alleviated partially by having the singers sing the lines as if the dot were a rest ♪ ₇♪ (♫₇♪) .

There is usually enough of an echo to make the sound appear continuous while the singers get the correct feeling for the sixteenth note.

There is the ever-present problem of forcing the singers into improper singing techniques when a new tone quality is asked for. This has been evident in a number of high school choruses I have seen, whose directors attended a college or university which was famous for a particular tone quality. Generally, these colleges or universities had advanced choirs whose members were chosen for a specific type of voice. The vocal technique was already established, and the choir was selected from a large pool of trained voices. High school directors are seldom this fortunate. The available singers are on the average moderately untrained, and to force a specific tone quality on these singers without adequately preparing them for it would be to risk damaging their voices. It must be emphasized, however, that with sufficient training there is almost no tone quality which is not obtainable from a high school chorus. The key words here are *moderation* and *training*.

The opposite end of the vocal spectrum would be the music of the Romantic period and particularly the music from Germany and Russia. Much of the more familiar music of the nineteenth and twentieth centuries is of a type which often requires sheer power and size for its full realization. Most of the music of the Russian school of religious music (Gretchaninov, Bortniansky, Kopylov, and others) is chordal. The emphasis is usually on the vertical, harmonic aspects, and because of this emphasis you should concentrate on what is happening at a given instant rather than on what is happening as a melody (horizontally). The homogenized sound is preferable for this type of music. The voices should be full, rich, and unified from top to bottom. In other words, the opposite of the Renaissance sound.

In the rehearsal, you may have more trouble with intonation than with the thinner, varied timbres. The vibratos may be more pronounced, with the result that some voices, particularly the basses, tend to sing slightly below the pitch. This flatness of pitch will not be readily discernible to the singers, but at the end of the piece the pitch will have sagged considerably. This is the type of music which benefits the most from rehearsing in a scrambled or integrated arrangement. If the music is not of excessive difficulty, you might even have the singers read the music the first time in this mixed seating. If they react in an average manner they will prefer this type of sight-reading. Besides building confidence and sight-reading ability, it will also give the singers keener pitch discrimination.

This thicker, more romantic sound has another built-in hazard; it is much more emotional in the commonly accepted meaning of the term. The music of the pre-Bach eras was also emotional, but much of it was of a stylized, frozen emotion, more in keeping with an intellectual approach to the music and text. "O let me die for true love" (Thomas Tomkins' madrigal) is hardly the same as "Arise, ye people, free and brave, defend our fair and native land" (Prokofiev, *Alexander Nevsky*). In the highly charged atmosphere of a large group of singers singing full tilt on a text of a patriotic or superemotional nature, there will be a decided tendency to wallow in the sound. This may tranquilize the singers' senses of pitch, attack, release, and pronunciation exactness. This is a good time for using the double-choir rehearsal technique in which half of the chorus sings and half listens. There is less of a tendency to become involved with the physical sound while listening and following a score. Also, the singers will be much more critical of the singing of their peers. Intonation and pronunciation will be gone over with a very fine nit-picking comb by the half-choir not singing.

I have found it best not to use a recording of a professional chorus to demonstrate tone quality. Sixteen-year-old beginning singers should not try to sound like 30-year-old experienced singers. However, it is still useful to have one section listen to another section and attempt to mirror the *color* of the sound. When a rich, full sound is wanted, it is probable that the altos and basses will have the tone color more nearly correct. Have the sopranos and tenors listen to a unison line by the altos and basses (particularly in the lower half of their ranges), and then try to duplicate this sound in their own range. There is an obvious danger in this procedure: *the singers may tighten their throats to get what they consider to be the correct sound, or they may alter the pronunciation drastically.* When using this technique, you must notice each voice individually and not consider the singers only by sections. If a head goes back unnaturally, or a jaw juts out, or some tightness appears around the mouth, begin working on basic singing and breathing techniques. The romantic sound is by far the easiest to produce with a relaxed jaw and open mouth, but first the singers must have the concept firmly in their minds. Certainly some vowels can be modified slightly to alter the sound, but basically the sound comes from the idea which is in the singers' minds.

In rehearsing a basically chordal work, watch for: (1) intonation problems, and (2) boredom. The first is often caused by the second. Boredom can be present even with a stimulating text. Boredom, in the choral vocabulary, is whatever lulls the singers from concentration on the mechanics of the music. Constant singing of one style of music can do this, so variety, either real or artificial, must be injected into the rehearsal. One method of learning the music without realizing it is to rehearse two parts at a time. In basically chordal music the text is approximately the same for all parts, so the words can be memorized even if the singer is silent. Separate the four sections so they sit or stand in four different parts of the room and rehearse two sections of the choir for the first half of the number, then have the remaining two sections finish. Or, to keep them on their mental toes, after a few measures of the altos and tenors singing, say "Altos drop out, basses begin," then in another two or three measures say "Tenors drop out, sopranos begin." This is a variation on the two-choir rehearsal.

The summation of this discussion on tone and compositional style is that you, as a choral conductor, must determine whether the composer wanted sound for sound's sake (where the tone quality is to be a thing of beauty in itself) or whether the composer wanted the sound to be such as to illustrate and clarify the construction (to make his musical intentions plainer). In other words, you must determine whether the music is subjective or objective. There is brass band music which is thrilling, although the music is brutally simple. There is also brass band music which is austere and stark to an extreme. You tell nothing by merely describing music as sounding like "a brass band," although there is a hackneyed, Sunday-afternoon-in-the-city-park tradition of brass band music. Choral music is the same. Adapt the tone quality to the music. Some music is impossible to realize fully with a high school choir. Russian liturgical music for male choir often has bass parts which never get up to the bass staff. High school boys might grunt out some of the notes but it would be unusual to find enough boys in a given high school to balance such a group.

One important note on rehearsing any music, whether homophonic or polyphonic: *try not to rehearse a single line at any time.* As much as possible have another section sing with the section having trouble. The parts must have a relationship to each other, and to have them played or sung alone gives an artificial and untrue picture. If two parts are having trouble, take them separately with one of the remaining two parts which are having an easier time of it. For instance, if the altos and tenors are having trouble, but the sopranos and basses are relatively sure of their parts, have the altos and sopranos sing the problem area, then have the altos and basses do the same thing, and finally have the altos, sopranos, and basses together. The same procedure should follow with the tenors singing first with the sopranos, then with the basses, and finally with both the sopranos and basses together. The accompanist should play the line causing the trouble and ignore the other line, unless there are some minor problems which could benefit from accompaniment. When the two troublesome parts can sing with the easier sections, have them sing together in two parts, alto and tenor, then alto, tenor, and bass, and finally all four parts. In this way at least half of the chorus is singing at all times, all parts get a chance to practice, and the sections having trouble have a gradual introduction to the sound of the remaining sections. See Chapter 9 for further suggestions on the part rehearsal.

This same technique of gradually adding parts can be used with polyphonic music, although there may occasionally be a problem of finding a good place to begin. With two parts it is not as much of a problem as finding a place for all four parts to begin. When entrances overlap, as in the point-of-imitation technique of most Renaissance motets and madrigals, you may have to start several measures back to get a running start at a section.

The Size of the Chorus

The actual rehearsal problems of the very large and the very small chorus will be covered in Chapter 11. At this point we can merely examine some of the reasons for using different-sized choruses.

The chamber choir movement is a relatively recent phenomenon in the United States. There have always been small choruses of from eight to 20 voices, but in the past few years there has been a remarkable rise in the number of institutions sponsoring chamber choirs, madrigal singers, solo ensembles, and the like. The problems in rehearsing these small groups have often been in the type of music chosen. All choral music is no more applicable to a small chamber ensemble than all instrumental music is applicable to a string quartet.

There are a number of elements which enter into the choice of music for a small or a large chorus. One of the most important is the choice of text. A small group of singers will probably be much closer physically to the audience and can present a song on more personal terms than a group of 200 standing on risers up on a stage. The text of Mendelssohn's *Im Walde* (*In the Wood*) says "You birds, trembling in the branches, how happy and free you are. I feel in my heart sick when I hear you from down below." A large chorus could sing this text, but it lends itself more readily to a chamber ensemble. On the other hand, a text such as "Arise, ye throngs, and trample the invaders" just does not fit a group of 12 high school singers. As a rule of thumb, it is best to remember that anything which would sound most natural spoken by a large group of people should be sung by a large group of people, and anything best spoken by a single person or a very few people in conversation will probably be performed best by a small group of singers.

The size of the original performing group can also alter the ideal size of the chorus. Renaissance music was often performed by soloists. Bach's choruses were performed by small groups. Handel's oratorios were performed by nothing like as large a group as some of the festival choruses now in existence. Much of the "choral" music of the nineteenth century was written for performance by soloists. An historical knowledge of the various types of concerted vocal music is an absolute must for performance of any music.

Some internal evidence as to the suitability of a piece of music for a large or small chorus is in the texture (thick or thin, slow or fast moving harmonies), the dynamics (sustained loud singing, the use of extreme dynamics for their own effect), divided sections, and excessive ranges (which usually indicates a particular sonority not easily obtained by a small group).

The reason for investigating this area is to prevent the choosing of music which will be unnaturally difficult to rehearse. Trying to get a large chorus to sound convincing on a text such as "Ah, let me die for true love" is much more difficult than a simple mixed quartet or possibly a dozen singers. The notes can be learned, but the emotion is unnatural for a large group.

There will be less of a problem in getting music which is too "big" for a chamber choir. Unless the group is amplified, it will become obvious quickly that a large patriotic flag-waver is not the proper choice for a dozen high school voices. However, it may not be as obvious in rehearsal that a piece of music from the Russian school of religious music which divides into ten parts is improper for a group of 20 singers. The rehearsal may emphasize having all of the notes sung in tune, but it may not be until a program leaves an audience unmoved that you realize the music demands more than tuned notes.

Choral Tone

As was mentioned earlier in this chapter, there are very real dangers in describing how specific tone qualities should be obtained. Each singer has different abilities and problems, and each director has different abilities and training. To ask for a "straight" tone means different things to different choruses and directors. In one case it might be a natural sound, and in another it might cause a tight, squeaky sound. To ask for a rich sound could mean anything from a free, natural tone to a raucous, strident, shouted sound with a wide vibrato.

For these reasons, it is impractical for this book to give much technical advice on tone production. It is best to describe and contrast four basic tone qualities, and leave it up to the ability of the individual directors to experiment in getting the tone qualities.

For our purposes, we will divide the available tone qualities into four main groupings: (1) straight, (2) smooth, (3) rich, and (4) driven. As with any arbitrary grouping of several items, the terminology is open to debate. However, allowing for mutations and gradations within each division, these should help us determine the course of our rehearsal.

The *straight* tone means either no vibrato or an unnoticeable amount of vibrato. With young children this is the natural vocal sound, and with a small percentage of singers this remains into the adult years. Male singers can be taught to use the falsetto voice and the head voice (there are other terms for this latter type). Both of these are much "straighter" than the average natural voice. When asking for the straight sound, watch carefully for signs of strain or unnatural means of control. High school tenors are particularly susceptible to tight throats.

The *smooth* tone is the average tone of an average high school chorus of modestly experienced singers. There are some voices which are relatively straight and some which have developed some noticeable vibratos, but for the most part they average together into a smooth, blended group with similar characteristics from the top of the range to the bottom. This is a useable tone quality but by itself it is not very dramatic or interesting. An entire concert of pieces using this tone alone would be quite dull. It can be the basic sound from which all other tone qualities are derived. It can also be the sound used in sight-reading. There is absolutely nothing wrong with it, except when it is overused. A gentle folk song or a nondramatic setting of a religious text could use it quite well. It would not work as well for pre-1600 music or for music which is highly dramatic.

The *rich* tone will be the sound toward which your singers

should be guided. This is the controlled, mature sound with the depth and color of a professional choir. There is one basic qualification which must be stressed for this tone: *the singers must be able to both crescendo and decrescendo without losing the intensity and pitch.* Until this is achieved there is the ever-present possibility that the richness is coming from improper vocal production. The necktie tenor sound and the tone coming from an alto carrying the chest voice too high are the most prominent problems. These should be worked on during the warm-up period. The tenors and sopranos may be driven to create an unnatural sound which approximates the rich sound, by singing above their natural ranges.

The *driven* tone quality is only used for special effects and should under no circumstances become a norm. It is very dramatic, individual voices may occasionally be evident, and it quickly tires both the singers and the audience. It is actually a type of shouting on pitch, which has its place in singing just as a cymbal crash or a whack on a bass drum has its place in instrumental music. In rehearsing music which requires this type of singing be very sparing in its use during the actual rehearsal period. As with any rich flavor, it can become cloying rather quickly. Another danger is that it will become boring to the singers before the performance. This also applies to certain songs which have handclapping as part of the musical fabric. Instead of clapping with the full palm of the hand, have them use only two fingers slapping the other palm. This gives the same rhythmic effect, but it saves the full sound for the few last rehearsals and the performances where it will count more. When using the driven tone, rehearse with a rich tone or even with a completely bland tone. This makes the driven tone stand out in greater relief when it is used.

In the rehearsal period it is often useful to change the tone quality completely, even to an incorrect sound, in order to obtain a specific goal. Music which requires a rich or driven tone quality may be difficult to get in tune. In that case just ask for a smooth or even a straight tone, both of which are more easily tuned. It also may be useful to sing a gentle madrigal or motet at an extremely fast tempo and with a driven tone, to show the contrast between that tone and what it should actually be.

CHAPTER 8

Utilizing
Successful
Warm-Up
Techniques

One of the most valuable items in a rehearsal period is the brief time at the beginning when the voices are warmed up for singing. It is at this time that future tone quality and vocal control are taught and polished. The warm-up is much more than a time for clearing away vocal cobwebs; it is a time for concentration on physical muscle control (for proper breathing and facial movement) and on aural sensitivity (for proper pitch discrimination).

The exercises for this warm-up period must be changed periodically to remain in line with the advancing ability of the choir. There are a few basic exercises which work well throughout the life of the singer, but new exercises and scale patterns need to be introduced for freshness as well as to extend the singing technique. These new exercises can be devised by the inventive director to emphasize such concepts as singing broken chord patterns on major, minor, diminished, or augmented chords, on the various minor scales, on staccato passages, or on alternation of staccato/legato measures. While these exercises should not be so complicated that all of the concentration goes to finding and hitting the notes, it is still more interesting to both the singers and the director to have warm-up exercises which are worth doing correctly.

- **Note No. 1**: *if the director shows extreme interest in getting the exercises exactly right, the singers will usually show a similar interest.*

- **Note No. 2**: *a sense of humor by the director which shows him having fun with the exercises while still demanding accuracy will encourage the singers to have a better attitude toward these musical push-ups.*

A basic problem often overlooked in warm-ups is that the physical body must be warmed up as well as the vocal cords. Actually, there is no such thing as warming up the voice alone, since a good "voice" requires proper muscular control for sustained tone, pitch, and quality. The exercises must include this warming up of muscles which control the breathing apparatus. The earlier in the day the rehearsal occurs, the more important is this warming up of the muscles. An 8:00 A.M. rehearsal might require some minor calisthenics to get rusty muscles working. The reasoning behind this is that some breathing muscles might be impaired in performing their duties if other muscles allow the body to slump in some way, particularly if the singers are seated. It is not enough to say "Everybody sit up straight"; they have to have the mental and muscular tone to do so.

It should not be assumed that either the body or the "voice" will be warmed up for an afternoon or night rehearsal just because some talking or moving about has occurred. A night rehearsal can be as troublesome as a morning rehearsal. The day's fatigue may have been partly overcome by an evening meal and some relaxation, but the singers might be so relaxed that they will not or cannot make the body muscles perform properly. Also, talking will not necessarily warm up a voice. It may harm the voice but it will seldom help it. The reason for this is that an infinitesimal number of people speak properly; that is, with good breathing control and muscular coordination. This leaves the speaking to the control of the throat muscles, which in turn makes a voice higher in pitch, more raspy, and less controllable. An afternoon or evening rehearsal will require some of the same physical exercises to get the body in tune as a morning rehearsal.

For the sake of variety, and to keep the singers from falling into the habit of considering the warm-up as a thing to be endured, vary the order of warm-up exercises. These exercises will fall under four basic classifications: (1) muscular awakening, (2) range extending, (3) intonation practice, and (4) quality improvement. Included in the last mentioned would be purity of vowels, faster consonant pronunciation, and differentiation between vowels which feel the same to the singer but sound differently to a listener (*eh* as in *every*, contrasted with *aah* as in *cat*).

Muscular Awakening

One simple exercise has proven efficient in getting the diaphragm and breathing muscles working after a 23-hour layoff. Basically, it is a series of fast breaths and tone starts, since a new breath is taken for each note.

Figure 8–1

Because of its length, you will have time to observe several singers during the course of the exercise. As they take a new breath for each note, make sure that they are not singing with a staccato sound. If they are making each note staccato instead of a full eighth note, they may be singing with throat muscle control and giving each note a glottal attack. The sound must continue for a complete eighth note, then stop for a complete eighth rest. As much as possible there should be no accent on the beginnings of the notes. This will cut down on the tendency to use the throat to control the starting and stopping of the sound. If the singers persist in accenting the notes, slow the tempo drastically so they can phrase each note enough to be obvious, as in Figure 8–2.

etc.

Figure 8–2

One problem you will find is that on the decrescendo the singers will have a tendency to relax all breathing muscles. Early in their training it is best to keep the crescendo/diminuendo

($\prec\,\bullet\!\!\succ$) exercises relatively low in their range. As the

muscle tone develops, the exercises can be raised in pitch. It is an axiom that a singer does not have control of a note until he can both crescendo and decrescendo on that note with no loss of quality. Obviously, most singers can sing both higher and lower than their actual useable range, but the notes at the extremes are not in control because they cannot be made softer or louder without straining the wrong muscles. The warm-up is the time when these extreme notes are trained into submission.

Of the two dynamic changes, the diminuendo is by far the most difficult to teach, probably because it is so seldom demanded of a singer. If you have any kickback from the singers, or if they appear unconvinced that such is necessary, get a recording of a string quartet by Mozart, Mendelssohn, or Brahms and play the slow movement. Basic musicianship prevails in all music, whether for strings, winds, or voices. The singers should be able to hear that all notes are not of equal importance and that a note does not always consist of a sharp attack and a brutal cutoff (Figure 8–3),

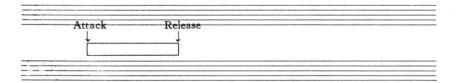

Figure 8–3

but that the more normal sound is the "football-shaped" sound (Figure 8–4).

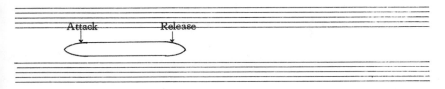

Figure 8–4

Musically this would appear as in Figure 8–5.

Figure 8–5

This concept of phrasing each note must be instilled in each singer to keep the music from becoming blunt and formless. A simple exercise for this decrescendo is shown in Figure 8–6.

(Slow Diminuendo)

Figure 8–6

This is a quick exercise which accomplishes two fundamental goals: (1) the major triad is sung with varying dynamics on both the third and fifth of the chord, thus forcing the singers to stay on the proper pitch throughout dynamic changes; and (2) the final note has a long, slow diminuendo which must be performed

smoothly. Make sure the singers perform this as ══ and not

as ══ . It is much easier to make a *subito piano* volume

change and then hold the softer dynamic.

There are various exercises for getting the major muscles of the body to respond. These are actually basic calisthenics often used in physical education classes but which can be used in choral rehearsals for their awakening qualities. Every book on vocal and choral technique has a listing of several different methods. The following are not original by any means, but they have been found to be effective.

"Boxing" is just that, a bouncing on the balls of the feet while making straight thrusts with the arms. This gets the muscles in the upper trunk unlimbered. These are the main breathing muscles, without which the singers will find themselves gasping for short two-measure breaths.

Raising the arms over the head does somewhat the same thing as boxing, in that the muscles in the trunk area are stretched. Particularly affected are the muscles which control the rib cage and keep it in place during normal breathing. While the arms are raised, have the singers exhale and inhale twice at moderate speed (any faster and they may become light-headed).

Bend at the waist and swing the arms from side to side like a pendulum. This works on the waist and back muscles.

If space on the risers permits, you might try shallow knee bends (going only halfway down) or a modified exercise consisting of reaching as high as possible and then bending to touch the knees with the fingertips. This works on both waist and diaphragm muscles.

In order to get their minds awake, have everyone turn to the right and rub the neck and shoulder muscles of the person who is then standing in front of them. This doesn't help the muscles as much as it causes giggling and conversation, which in turn awakens some sluggards. Have them turn 180 degrees and do the same thing. This will work in any rehearsal, but it is particularly valuable when the singers have an afternoon rehearsal after a dull day of classes.

Have them place the heels of their hands together and push. This isometric-type exercise also works on the chest muscles. Hooking the fingers together and pulling or jerking does the same thing.

The younger the singers, the more important these exercises become. Most beginning singers are unaware that muscle tone and pure work are connected with singing. Singing a rich pianissimo can be a very tiring job, and the earlier they learn the technique the better.

Insensitivity to Vowel Changes

Many singers do not hear the difference between certain vowels while they are singing. They are, for practical purposes, tone-deaf to the change when going from the *ee* of *steep* to the *eh* of *step*, or from *eh* in *bet* to the *aah* in *bat*. It is within the realm of the warm-up, to give the singers this aural sensitivity to distinguish between closely related sounds and the technical ability to sing the difference. Because of regional dialects, each director will have specific problems which will be more pronounced than others. Most regionalisms will need to be corrected for proper and unaffected choral singing. Most of these accents are due to improper vowel construction or inserting or removing diphthongs in certain words.

There is a school of choral technique which demands that only pure vowel sounds be used; that is, that no mutations be allowed. I have found that long-held notes should be treated in this manner. However, I have also found that to understand words sung by a chorus, it is necessary to hear changes in vowels or differences between vowels and consonants. Without changes there is no understanding. The word *my* consists of three sounds, *mmm*, *ah* (the dominant sound), and *ee* (this being very briefly sounded). Without all three sounds you have only *mmah*, which is not a word, although in some regions it substitutes for *my*. By no stretch of the imagination could we call it an accurate English pronunciation.

Some singers will not hear this final *ee* sound because they have never been taught that the word *my* contains three sounds, the last one being *ee*. Using a tape recorder will be a help, but you still may encounter some static from those singers who believe the three-sound pronunciation is blatantly wrong. Most dictionaries are useless, since these books habitually show the word pronounced as *mī*, as in *ice, rice,* or *dice*. In areas where these are pronounced as *aahs* (to rhyme with *glass*) or *daahs* (to rhyme with *grass*), you will have trouble at first. The students' confidence in your judgment is about all that will have an eventual effect. Of course, I have on occasion heard choral directors, whose personal speech patterns were enough to make grown men cry. If they cannot hear their own mismanagement of our inherited language, how can they hope to convince others that such words as *my* has three sounds?

Tongue position is the key to vowel construction, and it is also the key to proper pronunciation. To facilitate their hearing the difference between vowels, the singers must be given simple exercises which present the problem vowels in alternation. The following special exercises force the tongue to do its proper work in differentiating between *ee* and *eh*.

EE EH EE EH EE EH EE EH

Figure 8–7

Be extremely careful that the singers do not sing *ee-aah* instead of a pure *ee-eh*. Certain regional accents make the word *led* into *laah-uhd*. These singers have been trained from infancy to hear in this manner, and it will take considerable work and enthusiasm on your part to get them to sing properly. In only a small number of cases will this knowledge carry over into the spoken language, which is a great misfortune. Some of the singers will, in fact, consider this new method of pronunciation actually a mispronunciation. The use of a tape recorder is helpful in convincing them that their pronunciation is not what they think they are speaking and hearing.

The same problem arises in the *aah* sound. For many years it was common to make all words like *land, sand,* and *bland* into *lond, sond,* and *blond* ("Lond where our fathers died"). Although this has been pretty well dispelled in most sections, the ability to say a proper *aah* (*sand*) is still not the common property of choral singers. Use the same exercise as Figure 8–7 but change the vowels to an alternation of *eh-aah* (rhyming with *bet-sat*), as in Figure 8–8.

This combination is more difficult for the singers to hear, so you must be more alert to problems of mispronunciations. Have

EE   AAH   EH   AAH   EE   AAH   EH   AAH   EE   AAH   etc.

Figure 8–8

each section of the choir sing alone the first time through so the rest of the choir may listen. When they have this *aah* mastered, alter the exercise to the following:

EE   EH   AAH   EE   EH   AAH   EE   EH   AAH

Figure 8–9

This allows the singers to hear the three brightest vowels in close order. For some singers it will be the first inkling that these vowels are not pronounced the same. Students with limited cultural backgrounds will probably have the most trouble, since they have not heard a variety of speech patterns.

The seven basic pure vowels are *oo* (*tool*), *oh* (*rope*), *aw* (*draw*), *ah* (*hot*), *aah* (*hat*), *eh* (*bet*), and *ee* (*tea*). Contrary to some teachers of the written word, there are more sounds required of a speaker or a singer than are contained in *a, e, i, o,* and *u*. These five letters actually have two pure vowel sounds (*e* and *o*), two diphthongs (*a* is actually made up of *eh-ee* spoken quickly, and *i* is *ah-ee*), and *u* which can be either *oo* or *ee-oo*. Your job as choral director will undoubtedly encompass that of a speech teacher, which means that you must speak all of the words aloud before you get to the rehearsal so you will recognize the problems which will crop up.

Diphthongs

As mentioned above, most regional accents are due to improper vowel choice, the placing of diphthong sounds where none should be, or removing half of an existing diphthong. By and large,

111

the consonants are not a problem, except where they simply are not pronounced or are added as part of a regional dialect. A *g* sounds the same on the East coast as on the West. *Frog* may be pronounced *frawg, frowg,* or *frahg,* but the difference is entirely within the vowel choice. One choral director recalled directing a chorus singing *Elijah Rock,* and instead of the opening words being "Elijah Rock, shout, shout," it came out "Elijah Rock, shoot, shoot."

One cure for the insertion of added vowels (making diphthongs where there are only single vowel sounds) is to choose words which use specific single vowels and hold them for a few seconds. This allows the singers to hear the first sound by itself. Some singers will try to go to the second vowel sound immediately. If they persist, leave off the final consonant in such a word as *let.* This keeps the sound on *eh.* It will come as a shock to some singers (and possibly to some directors) that there is no such single vowel sound as *ay* (may). It consists of *mā-ee,* and should be sung on the first vowel of the diphthong. It also might be mispronounced by some as *mah-ee* to rhyme with *my,* which is a total misrepresentation of the word. Use the following exercise to force the singers to kick the habit of incorrect vowels:

Figure 8–10

When they have the vowels absolutely correct, make the next step and have them sing the word as a legato two-syllable word.

Figure 8–11

Finally, sing two of the words, alternating fairly rapidly but still with both of the sounds present.

MAY SAY DAY SAY MAY SAY DAY etc.

Figure 8–12

This type of instruction will pay off in later rehearsals when you merely refer to the diphthong sound in words such as *rejoice* (*re-jaw-eese*), *voice* (*vaw-eese*), *fight* (*fah-eet*), *might* (*mah-eet*), *way* (*wā-ee*), and *today* (*too-deh-ee*).

Quality Improvement

This is far too involved an area to give much space to suggestions. However, there is one basic exercise which has worked to give a more mature sound. We are concerned with the open, rich, resonant sound of a well-trained adult voice. Coming from a green teen-age voice, this sound will be somewhat harsh and uncontrolled at first because the singer will probably not hear it accurately. In fact, many singers may not want the sound because it is more trouble to control than the smooth, bland "average" high school sound. Because this tone quality can be much louder and more resonant, they will have a brighter palette of tonal colors to work with, and thus they must exercise more discrimination. And so must you, as their director. The full, mature sound is a heady brew to work with. Beware of the temptation to choose music to show it off at the expense of a more varied program.

Basically the rich tone we are speaking of is the product of controlled nasal resonance. The problem comes in allowing *un*controlled or *over*controlled resonance to occur. No control results in a blatant, usually mispronounced series of words, while overcontrol may give a thin, bland sound. Both sounds may be useful in isolated pieces of music, but the basic tone quality should be one of modest resonance which can be increased or decreased at will. This ideal may not be realized thoroughly until college or even later, but it should most certainly be started in high school. Besides the artistic goal of better realization of the music, it has the added benefit of producing a much louder tone with no more effort on the part of the singers.

Choose a pitch in the middle of the range and have the singers go back and forth slowly between an *nn* sound (open lip hum) and a vowel.

NN - AW   NN - AW   NN - AW   etc.

Figure 8–13

Then have the singers place their fingers on the bridge of their noses to feel the buzzing resonance during the *nn* sound, and then have them retain this same buzzing sensation during the vowel sound. When they have this resonant, nasal vowel sound, have them keep their fingers on their noses and experiment in stopping and starting the resonance while sustaining the vowel sound. This should be practiced on all vowels, since each singer will have his or her own particular problems with the various sounds.

Obviously there are many other problems in the emerging high school voice, but the directors' vocal background should provide the answers to many of them, and through trial and error at least partial answers to the rest.

Intonation Practice

The warm-up period is no time to allow bad intonation to occur. True, the first two or three exercises at any rehearsal may sound like feeding time at the zoo, but after that you should demand that the voices sing the exercises in exact tune. For this reason, you should not restrict your exercises to the major mode. Not only can you use minor,

etc.

Figure 8–14

but also short artificial scale passages,

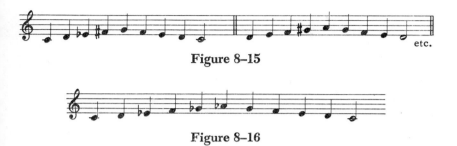

Figure 8–15

Figure 8–16

as well as diminished and augmented triads.

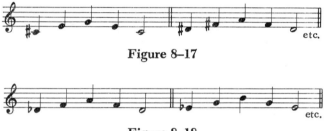

Figure 8–17

Figure 8–18

Note: *Through trial and error I have found that it is best to move the warm-up exercises up or down by a major second rather than the more common minor second.*

Figure 8–19

The voices can sing each succeeding major or minor mode exercise in tune much better when moving by a major second, probably because there are three common tones from one exercise to the succeeding one. When moving by a minor second, there is only one tone common to each succeeding exercise. There is a valid argument for moving by the minor second in that the singers must use greater discrimination in pitch. In advanced singers this may be true, but in the majority of high schools and particularly at the beginning of a rehearsal, it is asking a lot to require singers to: (1) use proper breath control; (2) get the right vowel position; (3) obtain properly controlled resonance; and (4) sing every note in correct intonation. In moving from a C major scale to a D major scale and finally to an E major scale (using only the first five degrees of each scale), you will find that the E remains constant through all three chords. This gives the singers something to hang on to, a sort of rock in a tonal wilderness.

As was mentioned previously, unless a singer has the ability to crescendo and diminuendo on a note, he does not actually have that note under control. In addition to being better musicianship in general, it is also valuable to have the singers make a practice of phrasing each note of any appreciable length. This means the note expands in volume without changing the pitch. One fine conductor calls this "expanding" the note. When the singers are working on the sight-reading sheets, you can slow down any exercise so each note is capable of being phrased. Many of the finest stringed-instrument players do this very thing—slow a passage to the point that every note can be played. It is irrelevant whether they can do it in a concert, they want to know how it might be played if they had the technical ability.

Some singers may balk at doing this because they find it more work than they had expected in singing. It requires a tremendous amount of physical energy. I had one mature singer of 30 years flatly refuse to sing some Schumann songs because she considered such singing mannered and false. I played a recording of two fine singers, one male and one female, both of whom phrased in exactly the manner I had suggested. Her answer was, "I don't care. It's not a vocal sound." Then I played some Schumann and Brahms string works where the musical phrasing was immaculate. Her answer: "See what I mean! That's instrumental phrasing, not vocal phrasing." She missed the entire point that phrasing is a musical characteristic and necessity, not something limited to specific instruments. Instructing the singers in the art of musical phrasing will improve both their intonation and overall musicianship.

Words for Tone- and Technique-Building

You should develop your own list of words which produce a particular tone quality or a specific vowel sound with your choirs. For instance, the word *living* sung several times on a single tone will force the singers to use a tonal *v* (with a definite, continual pitch) rather than the *f* sound which has no pitch. Singing this word in four sections, *lllll-iiiii-vvvvv-innnnnngggg*, will prove to the skeptics that *living* is a four-syllable, or at least a four-sound, word for singers.

Another word is the word *ruling*. The problem is that this word has four separate tones which must be produced and put in the proper pitch, *rrrrr-oooooo-lllll-innnnnngggg*. Unless the singers are aware that both the *r* and the *l* sounds have pitch, as well as the *oo* and the *ng*, they will slough off these consonants as relatively unimportant. If the singers do not give the individual parts their proper due, have them sing the word in the following manner:

RRR - OOO - LLL - INGG, RRR - OOO - LLL - INGG

Figure 8–20

Rather than make this exercise a part of your warm-up repertory for use at every rehearsal, wait until some similar word is being sung improperly, then make up a musical phrase with a note for each part. A word as apparently uncomplicated as *simply* will turn out to have six basic parts: *sssss-iiiii-mmmmm-puh-lllll-eeeee*. The *s* and the *p* will have no voiced sound, but the other four sounds will all have their pitch problems. This is one of the predominant reasons for a choir flatting. If the voices sing the darker vowels below pitch, they can only go down. The darker vowels (*oo, oh*) have a particular tendency to be on the flat side of the pitch, and the voiced consonants can sometimes be a

117

quarter-tone flat or sharp if they are sung without the knowledge that they have pitch.

Extending the Range

As was mentioned earlier in this chapter, a note is not in control unless the singer can both crescendo and diminuendo on it using any vowel sound within reason. Obviously, there will be more difficulty involved in having a soprano produce a high B-flat using an *ee* vowel than in producing a basic *ah* sound.

Almost any of the foregoing exercises can be used for range extension, with the proviso always in mind that *piano* and *pianissimo* singing is the final judge of whether or not a note is useable. The lower the dynamic level, the more energy the singers should put out.

The men, and particularly the basses, should be instructed quite early in the use of both the head tone and the falsetto. These are quite valid vocal qualities and are of great help to the choral director doing a variety of styles of music. Using the head tone, the basses can sing softly up to F's and G's without losing the intensity. Have them sing a sliding pitch up as high as they can without breaking over into a falsetto tone. Have them repeat this sliding tone (a tone without individual pitches) a number of times, each time at a lower dynamic level. You must be sure they do not tighten the jaw and throat muscles. When they appear to have this concept firmly in mind (they should be able to slide to a treble clef G or above), start at the G below middle C and have them sing major triads very lightly until they are singing at the upper limits. Most of your problem will be in their disbelief that they can do this singing in the musical ionosphere. Those boys who have just recently managed to sing low enough for the bass notes will be particularly reticent about returning to (as they might suppose) a more childlike voice. You can assure them the use of neither the head tone nor the falsetto will in any way impair their lower range.

For extending the range downward, a similar technique should be used, emphasizing to the singers that the *piano* and *pianissimo* dynamics are much more effective than loud singing.

Both the tenors and sopranos can and should work in the lower extremes of their ranges during the warm-up period. Besides getting the jaw loosened, it will add richness throughout the range.

One tone color often ignored is the chest register of the female voice. This is a loud, often raucous, sound which is difficult to control but quite useable in certain types of music. It gives the altos much greater power in the lower range. This register can be developed by singing the following exercise:

EE AW_____   EE AW_____   EE AW_____ etc.

Figure 8–21

Do not overdo this exercise, particularly at its first presentation. It is not so much a matter of developing the chest voice as proving to the girls that they actually have such a voice available. The main problem will be in controlling both the pitch and volume of this new voice.

CHAPTER 9

Fashioning Techniques for the Part Rehearsal

Some choral works, for one reason or another, require the polishing of separate parts which can only come about in a part rehearsal. As with any other rehearsal, there are right and wrong things to do in a part rehearsal. Further, there are different "sizes" of part rehearsals. Finally, do not expect results from a part rehearsal which are not within its scope.

It must be stated at the onset that having part rehearsals is neither an admission of poor technique with the whole chorus, nor is it something that is to be used with every piece of music. One well-known professional choral conductor begins every tour rehearsal with extensive part rehearsals. His feeling is that in this manner all of the individual sections can have a unity of sound and phrasing, which is impossible or unreasonably time consuming to work out in the full rehearsal. With the ever-present problem of 30 singers being paid by the hour, his feeling is that economics preclude his having two or three sections sitting around for five or ten minutes while one or two sections work on difficult passages. Another professional choral conductor prefers his part rehearsals by quartets, so he can find weak voices. This is a type of "part" rehearsal often overlooked.

What a Part Rehearsal Does Best

A part rehearsal performs three basic functions: (1) it obtains a blend within sections which is difficult and time consuming within the framework of a standard rehearsal; (2) it teaches melodic segments which are beyond the technical ability of the choir to hear while singing three- or four-part music; and (3) it teaches phrasing and basic musicianship which might be overlooked or ignored in the full rehearsal. Beyond these three, there is little a part rehearsal can accomplish. It cannot obtain a blend between sections unless the part rehearsal consists of more than one part. In highly dissonant music, the rehearsal of a single part will be helpful but not totally successful until another part is put beside it for reference.

With a green choir, a part rehearsal may be most valuable in gaining a blend within each section. Individual voices will be much more apparent in a group of 15 basses singing by itself than in a group of 50 or 60 diverse voices. It is obvious that a part rehearsal should not be considered as limited to picking out notes. When a single section is isolated, you can devise exercises which are specifically aimed at correcting that one section's problems. Each section may have different tendencies; the basses may lean toward muffled vowels, the tenors toward throaty sounds, the altos toward harsh consonants, and the sopranos toward screeching high notes. You can waste a lot of time in the full rehearsal attacking each of these in turn.

Allied with the teaching of proper blending is the teaching of phrasing and musicianship by each section. This is of particular importance in contrapuntal music where the individual note stresses will fall at different points in the piece. Once the concept of phrasing is instilled in the group, you will generally only need to mention a key word or phrase to have a section perform its part properly, but trying to work this out in a full rehearsal can be excruciatingly time consuming. And time conservation is the name of the game.

Even the teaching of notes has particular techniques which help the singers to hear certain intervals. It is not a matter of playing a passage on the piano and then having the singers echo this phrase (although some passages may require this time-honored technique). The part rehearsal can be a time when small helps and hints can be given to each section concerning certain problems which are inherent within each classification of voice.

Blending the Voices

You can make a part rehearsal do double duty by working on blending while learning notes. Except in passages which have awkward syllabification or very rapid word changes, the text will not be a great stumbling block. The text can usually be learned (but not necessarily memorized) in the full rehearsal without any special emphasis. For this reason, it is useful during the part rehearsal to give at least some of the time to singing on the various vowel sounds, particularly those which are most often mispronounced, *aah* (as in *hat*) and *oo* (both *boot* and *foot*). All voices are susceptible to the problem of changing the basic vowel sound as they move from one part of their range to another. Rehearsing a section with one vowel will isolate these problems and make the singers more aware of their own sounds, particularly if half of the section sings while the remaining half listens to a problem area. This problem most often occurs at one or another of the extremes of range or dynamics.

At this point we must discuss one major choral sin: the *disappearing vowel*. Words which contain two consecutive vowel sounds may be sounded on either of the vowel sounds, but as a rule there should be no gradual change from one vowel to the next. This gradual change is what is usually termed a "disappearing vowel." Inexperienced singers are so taken up with pitch and rhythm problems that often they never hear their own vowel sounds. A tape recorder will help prove to them that they actually are allowing some vowels to melt into the next. Because the individual sections will have only one line to hear, the part rehearsal is an excellent time to work on these disappearing vowels.

Do not be afraid to use particularly ill-sounding vowels such as a nasal *aah* or an acid *ee* if it will stretch the singers' understanding of the large number of sounds available to the chorus. Also, and this is of prime importance, the brighter vowels are much more easily tuned than *oo*'s and *oh*'s. If the singers have trouble hearing each other, have them stand in a small circle so the sound goes into a common melting pot. A variation of this is to have them stand grouped in a corner where the sound can reverberate off the two walls. This usually works better with a group of a dozen or less. There is, of course, the possibility that the acoustical characteristics of a particular room may keep this technique from being too successful.

In the final analysis it is you, the choral director, telling the exceptional (nonblending) voices to modify the sound in some way that gets the proper blend. It just happens to be easier in a part rehearsal.

Teaching Individual Notes

The traditional function of a part rehearsal is to teach the singers troublesome passages. This does not mean only those contemporary works with apparently no specific key, but also traditional tonal works from all musical eras. Renaissance motets and madrigals can have rhythmic and syllabification problems which are not easily worked out. They may become more apparent in part rehearsal, particularly if some hemiola rhythmic concepts (alternation of stresses in 6/8 and 3/4) were used by the composer. The long melismata of the late Baroque era are particularly helped by part rehearsals.

In teaching music as a line (horizontal, melodic), you will have to determine the various points of stress. These come either with a rhythmic accent (as with all first beats, most third beats in 4/4, fourth beats in 6/8 or 6/4, and so forth) or with an implied harmonic accent which may appear as a key tone after an altered note or by a skip of a fourth or fifth. These stressed notes become the main notes around which the other notes move. This concept is particularly important in such a musical line as Figure 9–1.

Figure 9-1

If you reduce the line to its diatonic notes, you have the following:

Figure 9-2

The three altered notes are then treated as ornamental notes. Have the singers perform Figure 9-2, then one at a time add the altered notes. By learning the diatonic notes first, there will be less of a tendency to stray from pitch.

Admittedly some music defies this type of learning process. A series like Figure 9-3 may be helped by breaking up the melody into smaller, more easily handled units.

Figure 9-3

All this does is give a tonic feeling to small sequences of notes, Figure 9-4 being a G-sharp minor chord, 9-5 has a pickup note into a B-flat minor chord, and 9-6 has the upper four notes of a B major scale.

Figure 9-4

Figure 9-5

Figure 9–6

Teach these in reverse, that is, 9–6, then 9–5 and 9–6 together, and finally all three in order. The singers should have no trouble with this sequence. The *best* method is to teach your singers to sing all intervals instantaneously, but this is an idealistic goal which is seldom attained in the average high school.

When learning a long melismatic passage from a Baroque work, take the line very slowly and then very fast. This helps break up the singers' relating the new music with other remembered pieces in the same style. All Handelian choruses do not sound like the *Messiah* choruses, but inexperienced singers do not know this and may inadvertently use the same sequences and melodic formulas. When using the piano with the part rehearsal, have the accompanist play every other note, and finally only those notes on strong beats. In Figure 9–7, play only the notes marked with an arrow. Because the passage is entirely diatonic the singers should have no trouble with the notes occurring between arrowed notes, and they may in fact not need this much piano help.

Figure 9–7

Note: *When playing a single line, as in a part rehearsal, play in a different octave than the one being sung. If the men are singing, play in the treble clef. If the women are singing, play either an octave above or below (if you need more volume, play both above and below). This octave transposition gives a different fundamental note for the singers' comparison with their own note and allows them to hear much more accurately. It is much easier than listening to their own octave, particularly for the alto and bass sections.*

Phrasing and Basic Musicianship

There is nothing to be said here except "do it." Demand proper attacks, releases, crescendos and diminuendos, articulation and legato singing, and particularly the observing of note lengths.

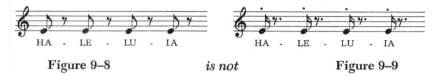

| Figure 9–8 | *is not* | Figure 9–9 |

There is a great difference in the intensity of the two illustrations, but this difference may be lost or ignored in working through a full rehearsal with all sections singing. In a part rehearsal, it will stand out in greater relief.

One of the most difficult musical requirements to realize is a long diminuendo on one note, particularly if some other section is doing something more interesting musically. If the tone is held so long that some or all of the singers have to take a new breath, then the felony is compounded because of the re-entrance of the voices. Have the singers practice coming in more softly than the existing voices and then bringing the volume up to what is already present in the other voices. Otherwise there will be a "blip" when they enter.

Two Sections at a Time

A variation on the part rehearsal is to have two sections rehearse at a time. This has the disadvantage of making one section wait if it is an absolute necessity that the other section work on a difficult place. However, in actual practice this is very seldom the case. Few choral works, particularly those which will be used by a high school chorus, will be so complicated that they will be unsingable using two sections at a time. A definite advantage of the two-section part rehearsal is that each section gives the other some tonal help. It becomes more of a three-dimensional work with the added voices.

If one section strikes a difficult passage, have the other section hum or sing a neutral vowel while the section with the problem sings the words. This gives enough difference to the individual sections to keep them from blurring together. Another method of two-part rehearsing is to have one section sing one vowel (*oo* or *oh*) while the other section sings a brighter vowel (*ee* or *eh*). This last-named technique is effective in music where the two parts move more or less together. Singing on contrasting vowels has the effect of making them sound like two different instruments and thus making each more easily heard.

If you have a regularly scheduled time for part rehearsals, use different combinations of voices—Alto/Tenor, Alto/Bass, Soprano/Tenor. Be careful that you do not always use only the women or only the men. One director made a practice of assigning one section to one student director and another section to a second student director, while he kept the remaining two sections. He directed a one-night-a-week civic chorus which met for two and one half hours. The first four or five rehearsals had a standard format of 45 minutes for a rehearsal of the full chorus, then 45 minutes of part rehearsal, a short break, then the remaining 45 or 50 minutes were for the full chorus rehearsal. He always had a list of problem passages with approximate times to spend on each which he gave to his student directors, so there was never a question of merely picking out random notes. In this way, he could get a lot of mileage out of one evening rehearsal. The average high school period of 50 or 55 minutes is too short for this three-section rehearsal. However, having part rehearsal for the first half and a full rehearsal for the concluding half can be profitable *if* the other rooms for rehearsing are not too far away. Sometimes the minutes spent in transit from a distant room can offset the time saved in part rehearsal.

If you use student directors for part rehearsals, be sure that they: (1) can play at least one line on the piano with decent facility or they have a pianist with them; and (2) have a list of passages to work on. Never assume that a singer knows all of the problem areas just because he or she happens to sing in that particular section. It might prove best to use a director from another section. It will also be helpful if the student director (or the accompanist) can transpose the one vocal line at sight. This is particularly helpful to the tenors and sopranos if the tessitura is consistently high. It is also helpful to the basses and altos if the tessitura is very low. This latter observation is often overlooked because it is assumed that the low voices sing better in their low range. Actually, they may hear more inaccurately in the low range, and transposing the melody up a whole tone may clear up some sticky intonation problems. This is particularly true if they have worked on a section several times and are consistently singing flat.

Short Part Rehearsals

One of the best aspects of a part rehearsal is that it can be scheduled in an otherwise useless time segment; such as a 20- or 25-minute study hall after or before lunch, or even as part of a split period if you can work it out with the principal. Even 15 minutes is valuable, if you can get all or most of the singers in a section to arrive promptly and you do not waste a minute. Fifteen minutes of hard work on the problems of one section can be as valuable as a full hour rehearsal to that section because there will be no singing of music already half-memorized just so other sections can practice.

Every school has scheduling problems which require certain classes, particularly physical education classes, to be given an ad hoc study period every few weeks. These often occur when an assembly is scheduled and the gymnasium has equipment set up in it. This may prevent the students from attending a gym class, but it also may provide you, the choral director, with a chance for a part rehearsal if you happen to have some students in that particular class. If you can't get a full section, take what you can get and work with those. It may be possible to get a quartet, in which case you can work on intonation or pronunciation by the individual voices. It takes a bit of planning ahead, but it is worth it. Although the students may gripe at the extra work, they will still appreciate (silently) your desire to have a top-drawer singing group.

Four-Part Part Rehearsals

Singing by quartets is a guaranteed method of spotting faulty intonation and pronunciation. Only in this way can some singers be convinced that they are hanging below the pitch, or sharping as they sing an ascending scale, or flatting a third of a chord. Selecting a quartet at random for a part rehearsal is much easier than trying to get every member of an 18-voice alto section together at one time. When working with a quartet, don't select the most difficult music or the most demanding passages for work. Quartet rehearsals are most valuable for improving the two aspects of choral singing listed above, intonation and pronunciation. As was mentioned earlier in this chapter, ask of a part rehearsal only what it can do the best.

If the singers need an added bit of stimulation to perform well in the quartet, tell them you are giving them evaluation points toward their semester grade. Then do it. If you can listen to them twice or three times a semester, even if for only five or ten minutes, it will be valuable.

CHAPTER 10

Coordinating the "Nonchoral" Rehearsal

Unless you try to make a career out of unaccompanied choral music, you will find yourself with a rehearsal of instruments or soloists from outside your choir. The person who said "Directing a chorus and directing an instrumental group is exactly the same," obviously had never directed both on the high school level. On the professional level, the anonymous speaker may be more correct. If everything in a piece of music automatically fell into place, if the intonation and pronunciation were always correct, if the soloists always knew their parts, then this chapter would be useless. But it isn't and they don't, so the following will prove helpful.

Conducting Technique

The actual conducting technique should stay pretty much the same from instrumental to choral conducting. Two of the most notable differences when directing amateurs will be in the facial expression and the use of the left hand. With instruments, the facial expression gives cues and some general characteristics.

With a chorus, the face mirrors the words more often than not. In instrumental directing, the left hand does what the right hand cannot do in the way of giving cues, indicating dynamics and articulation, and turning pages. The choral director's left hand gives the endings of words, beats time, phrases, and also does some of the work mentioned in this paragraph concerning instrumental conducting.

Choral directors do not always use the best conducting technique, possibly because much of their rehearsal time is taken up with working on pronunciation, vowel construction, dropped consonants, and other specifically choral problems. They just forget to do the time-beating in the proper manner. Also, choral music is often less involved rhythmically than band or orchestral music. There is a less pressing need for a strict, metronomically correct beat, so the beat patterns tend to become less exact as far as the traditional patterns are concerned. This is no problem to the choir because the singers are used to the pattern, or at least to the type of hand signals used by the conductor.

The problems of conducting technique arise when the conductor appears before a group of instrumentalists who are used to a standard beat pattern. If they see a pattern that attempts to cue the rhythms (for instance, all of the eighth notes in 4/4) instead of outlining the fundamental meters, there will be a severe lack of exactness. Then, when the conductor changes his style to a more readable pattern for the instrumentalists, the singers may find themselves leaving off final consonants, mispronouncing vowels, and doing other choral transgressions because the conductor is not reminding them of every small detail. This is another argument for a more correct beat pattern while directing a chorus; the singers may become far too dependent on signals from the director instead of relying on their own memories and training.

It is a common situation to have the chorus prepared before beginning rehearsal with the instrumentalists. For this reason, you should be ready to give almost all of your attention to the instrumental music, giving the chorus or soloists cues for entrances but not much more for the first rehearsal. Only when you have the proper style and solid ensemble among the instrumentalists should you return to the chorus. If the singers do not phrase correctly, or if a final consonant is dropped, or a vowel is sung incorrectly it is no great loss on an early rehearsal. It is, however, a problem if the chorus does not enter properly or if an instrument plays in the wrong key. Get the biggest problems out of the way first, then work on details.

If possible, work with the instrumentalists before bringing on your singers. The addition of the chorus is the same as beginning a rehearsal in front of an audience. The players will be more on edge, and this will be most pronounced when the instrumental group consists only of soloists. It is easier to become lost in a group of eight clarinets than if you are the only player on first clarinet. Allow for nervousness on their part the same as on yours. Ignore some mistakes and try for a complete read-through. If there are problems with rehearsal numbers, poor manuscript, or other bothersome but time-consuming details, it is better to get these out of the way before rehearsing with the singers.

Get the music to the players before the rehearsal if possible. Even a glance through the music will be helpful. If the trumpeter on a Bach cantata realizes he will have to have a good lip for the high tessitura, he will appear in a better frame of mind than if you suddenly spring the work on him after two hours of marching band rehearsal.

There is no way to estimate how much rehearsal time you will need for a given work. The length of the work, past experience, size of the group, difficulty of individual parts, and your own conducting ability will show whether two 30-minute rehearsals with the instrumentalists will be enough, or whether you will need every afternoon for a week to get the work into decent shape.

Rehearsal Numbers and Letters

When you anticipate performing a work with instruments, early in the rehearsal schedule begin using rehearsal numbers and measure numbers to designate a specific passage rather than the more common page/score/measure method for choral octavos. If your choral scores do not have rehearsal letters or numbers, use the time in early rehearsals to write them in. That is the time to find out, not when you have a group of instrumentalists sitting and waiting to rehearse. It would be a help to have the singers number all of the measures, beginning anew for each major division. This method eliminates the problem of searching for different rehearsal letters. However, it will also require the instrumentalists or a librarian numbering the measures of the individual instrumental parts.

Whether you use rehearsal numbers, or letters, or only the numbered measures, make it a habit to describe places beginning with the largest division and going to the smallest. Thus, in calling for a passage say "Trumpets, after letter R, measure one, two, three, four, omit the slur." In this manner, you have gone logically from the specific instrument to the basic division (letter division), then to the measure, and then you give the information about that measure.

Begin using the full score early in the choral rehearsal. Besides getting the feel of turning the larger pages and getting the pages to lay flat, you learn to describe places by the method suggested in the previous paragraph. Also, you can check wrong notes in the choral score, correct wrong rehearsal numbers, and adjust the volume, pronunciation, and/or tone quality in passages with thick orchestration. Using only a choral score which says *piano* in a passage without telling the accompanying forces, may lull both the conductor and the singers into singing too softly. It may be necessary to upgrade the dynamic level to *mezzo-forte* or above according to the number and type of instruments playing.

When You Have to Start Over Again

When rehearsing with an instrumental group, you will have a problem that is somewhat different than with only a piano as an accompanying instrument. You will need to return to specific passages for pinpoint rehearsal, just as with unaccompanied music. The instrumentalists can begin in the middle of a measure or even in the middle of a beat on a dissonant chord, but the singers need to have a pitch before they can sing. You will find it helpful to mark in your score places where most of the rehearsing will be likely to occur. Then find the most logical spot to begin that passage. You may need to back up two or three measures to locate a decent chord for starting the singers.

In polyphonic music this is particularly difficult, and thus particularly important. It *may* be necessary to go back ten or 12 measures to find a good beginning spot. It is a good idea to have your accompanist around during the rehearsal with the instruments so he or she can give pitches. This accompanist already knows the best places for starting over since you will already have returned to that spot several times in the strictly choral rehearsal.

Beware of the temptation to always start at the beginning of a movement or section. A dozen measures of 4/4 at 72 beats a minute is 40 seconds any way you count it. A rehearsal is basically constructed of small chunks such as these.

Do You Need a Dress Rehearsal?

For some reason, probably due to the traditions of the theatre, some directors want a dress rehearsal the day before the concert. At this final rehearsal, they want everything to be exactly as it will be on the concert. While this may work with some choruses (junior high and below, in particular), it may be too much of an anticlimax for more mature singers. You will find yourself working to get everything right for the dress rehearsal instead of working toward the concert. If you are going to have a dress rehearsal, have it two or three days before the concert so you can work on small details right before the concert itself. There is a spirit and fire that should be reserved for the concert which may be lost if too much emphasis is given to the dress rehearsal. Don't worry about the passages they already know; work on the tough spots. These will be the beginnings of movements, places where the tempo changes abruptly, very rapid and very slow passages. Your time with the instrumentalists is far too valuable to waste on repeating easy, already learned sections.

Placing the Instrumentalists

There are traditional seating plans for both orchestras and bands, so your problems with the large groups will not be as acute as with small ensembles. With the large groups, the main problem may be that of having enough space on the stage or in the rehearsal hall. It is a sort of musical "gas" law that musical groups tend to expand to fill the available space in a rehearsal hall. This means that putting two groups in a rehearsal hall designed for one ensemble will find both groups being crowded. It may be impossible to get the singers on risers during the early rehearsals in the band or choral rehearsal hall. Instead of trying to move everything in the hall, just have the singers stand where they can see you and forget about complete sections for the first rehearsal or two. As you get used to the room and as the players and singers get used to each other, everyone will make minor adjustments which will give every singer a better position. Then, when you get onto the stage or out in the gymnasium or wherever the concert is to be staged, you can begin with the choral risers and set up the instruments according to the size and shape of the area which remains.

With a small group of players you will have more room to work with, but some instruments work better facing one way than another. Tradition has the violins on the conductor's left and the cellos on his right. Once, while directing a pit orchestra, I had to move the cellos to my left. It left them baffled for about three rehearsals. "We've never seen a conductor from this side" was their startling statement. Remember that the direction a brass instrument faces alters the tone as it is perceived by the audience. A French horn aimed toward the chorus is more muffled to the audience but considerably louder to the chorus. When first positioning the stands and chairs for a small ensemble, place them in roughly the same position they would have in an orchestra. Then if a problem occurs, you can move the chairs without much wasted motion. Ask the players for suggestions if they feel uncomfortable in their positions.

One point to remember about a small ensemble: *it will sound still smaller in front of a large chorus in an auditorium than in a bare rehearsal room.* The audience and the chorus will both absorb a lot of acoustical energy. Be prepared for this change in sound. Don't hold them back too much in rehearsal.

The Accompanist

Some school systems have wisely budgeted money for an accompanist for the choral groups. Unfortunately, this is not a universal practice. You will probably use a student accompanist. The best arrangement is to have a full-time accompanist, meaning one which does not sing with the particular chorus he or she is accompanying. It is much better to have the accompanist at the piano throughout the rehearsal instead of coming up to sing when the music does not need accompanying and then running back to the piano to pick out notes. In addition to furnishing the piano accompaniment when there is a separate piano part, the accompanist plays lines for part rehearsals and gives pitches. For the last reason alone, the accompanist should always be at the piano during rehearsals.

It may be that two or three proficient pianists consider it a point of pride to be the accompanist for your choir. At this point, your political and musical talents are put to the acid test. Rather than divide the music among the accompanists so that each one has a separate group of pieces to accompany, assign all pieces to all players, then use them a day or a week at a time. This will prove to yourself *and to the choir* which pianist should be the one to perform a given work at the concert. It will also show which pianist is not really all that interested in learning the music accurately.

Besides the ability to play the piano, the accompanist must have or develop fast reflexes and a feeling for your style of rehearsal. When you say "sopranos and tenors only," the accompanist must automatically go from the piano reduction to the vocal lines to play those two parts. Likewise you should show the accompanist the technique of playing an octave higher or lower when playing one line only. Transposition of one line is likewise helpful.

One problem you will run into, particularly in choral music from European publishers, will be the lack of a piano reduction. At this point, the accompanist can do one of three things: (1) write out a piano reduction, (2) learn to play all four or five lines at sight, or (3) play as many lines as possible. In polyphonic music it may be enough to give the entrances of the parts, and this is most true in point-of-imitation, motet-style works where each entering voice is a version of the first motive. In works with simple chord structure and slow harmonic changes there may be little need for more than the bass and one other part to be played after the first run-through.

The Soloist

It is best to rehearse the soloist separately before letting him or her sing with the chorus. The fundamental reason is that it saves a lot of time. It also saves the ego of the soloist, in that he or she does not need to be corrected in front of the choir. It may be that you will have several singers who might be competent on the same solo. In this case, you may want to have a group "soloist" rehearsal outside of regular rehearsal time. If the prospective soloists are not enthused enough to meet an extra rehearsal they probably do not want the solo for the correct reason. If there is no extra time, or if the solo is relatively brief, have the entire section sing the solo part. The second time through have half of the section sing the part, the third time the other half sings the part, and after that choose individual voices. This shows both you *and the rest of the choir* which soloist has the best voice.

It has been emphasized a number of times that the choir needs to understand why a particular soloist or accompanist is being used. Comparison between two soloists will prove your musical point. Popularity has a tendency to gloss over actual lack of talent. Also there is the ever-present possibility that a voice has improved to the point that it is better than the one you had originally chosen.

If you decide to bring in outside soloists, you should understand both the advantages and disadvantages of such a practice. Obviously, the soloists will have stronger and more accurate voices, since they will probably be older singers from a local college or from the community. This means you will not have to drill the solo parts into their ears. On the other hand, you may have more trouble getting them to take the tempos and dynamic levels you want. In fact, you may feel a bit reticent about suggesting any changes to them in the areas of pronunciation, scooping into notes, or wide vibratos. If you have chosen your soloists correctly there will be no problem here, but you may have a limited number of potential soloists so you must be on your guard. There is also a potential pitfall in having the chorus thinking, "Well, we have a singer who is as good as that one." A high school singer's critical facilities are not as developed as yours and you may hear abilities they do not hear. Prepare your students in advance for the particular sound you want them to hear. Tell them why a particular sound is better for a specific number. A little education may be a dangerous thing, but it's better than no education at all.

Pronunciation and Instruments

The style of pronunciation you employ when your choir is singing unaccompanied, or with only a piano for accompaniment, must be altered rather drastically when you include an instrumental ensemble also. The articulation of the instruments, particularly brass instruments, is much more explosive than vocal articulation. The adding of a nonpronouncing musical line (instruments or humming voices) tends to dilute the effect of the pronounced words. Your only recourse is to ask for more explosive consonants and exaggerated articulation from your choir. The only musical exception to this would be in basically two-choir writing where the instrumental and choral groups are constantly playing separately.

The singers will probably not understand the degree of added effort they will need to expend in order to pronounce a text so it can be understood over the sound of an instrumental ensemble, even if there are only five or six brass instruments. The sounds will be grotesque (to them) while you are rehearsing without the instruments or with only a piano reduction. There is no convincing answer to their disbelief that you could actually want such a sound. All you can do is just plow ahead and assure them that the first rehearsal with the instruments will prove you right.

Have the singers whisper the text very loudly. This gets them used to the idea of forcing the consonants and pronouncing the complete sound of every letter in every word. A phrase such as "where are you now" has a series of liquid sounds which will come out as total mush unless the singers are carefully taught that only by the change from sound to sound do we truly understand a text. The four words in this phrase just mentioned contain the following sounds: *Whhh* (breath explosion)—*eh—rr—ah—rr—yee—oo—nn—ah—oo.* The *r* sounds are particularly important in this sequence because of their harshness in relation to the surrounding sounds. Such sounds will carry above the instrumental sound. The voiced consonants, *l, m, n,* and others, will need to be emphasized.

The problem of pronunciation will be compounded when your chorus is singing with a large band or orchestra. Your carefully worked out dynamics will probably be scrapped for a standard mezzo-forte-and-above volume level. Unless your choral group numbers in the 100's the band will literally blow the singers into nonexistence. Sixty instrumentalists can cover a group of vocalists twice that number, unless the conductor keeps both groups under firm control. The exaggerated pronunciation will be a large factor in having them heard. A cautionary note: *don't take recorded performances as any guide for your own level of sound.* These are professional voices and players, and they have the benefit of perfect studios and fantastic equipment. A tape may be cut on as many as five or six channels and then mixed in the studio to the proper sound. When you perform the Christmas cantata in the gymnasium you won't have that kind of control.

The warm-ups you do before a stage production or before a concert with an instrumental ensemble must emphasize the pronunciation problems listed above. If they begin forgetting during the concert, purse your lips and then show your teeth to remind them to use their lips and teeth to pronounce the words more properly.

The Chorus for the Musical or Operetta

The rehearsal problems inherent to staged choral works, musicals, or operettas are related to those found when combining a chorus and an instrumental group. Even if your chorus is going to perform with an accompaniment of only one or two pianos, your rehearsal problems will be centered around making the words understood by the paying customers. The pronunciation must be emphasized at each rehearsal, so the singers understand that only through constant attention to consonants and vowel changes can they hope to get their message across.

Fortunately most musical choruses of the past two decades have emphasized using a chorus on a unison melodic line, with division into two or more parts only at strategic places where the instrumentation is quite thin. This saves trying to blast through a full pit band with a standard SATB scoring and amateur voices. From the first rehearsal, demand extreme pronunciation. Have the singers practice forming the words without making a sound. This gets them used to moving their facial muscles. Unless they have extensive stage experience (impossible in the average high school), this will cause some giggling and possibly even some embarrassment. It is better to get this phase of their development out of the way in the early rehearsals than to wait until they are on stage where the waste in rehearsal time is much more critical. Tell them to mouth the words as if they were communicating across a large, silent study hall; or as if they were speaking through a soundproof, plate-glass window. They will not want to open their mouths as much as they will need to because they will feel their faces have been deformed. Have one-half of the chorus perform for the other half to show them that they don't look all that bad. Your singers will need to be reminded that visual communication is a necessary part of every staged production. The audience will see the singers' mouths working in certain patterns and will understand words that might otherwise escape them.

If there is one basic rule in stage chorus performance it is, *don't try to be too subtle.* Very soft singing is usually lost to the audience. Unless a sound comes over the footlights, there is no point in making that sound. Keep the rehearsal volume at a fairly high level and emphasize exaggerated pronunciation. When the audience arrives, it will soak up a lot of acoustical energy. Depending on the auditorium, this will be a help or a hindrance. In a very live auditorium, it will probably improve the diction of the singers. In a dead auditorium, even more sound will be lost.

Teach your singers to "fake" their head positions so they are never singing toward the wings or up toward the loft. Their voices should never be more than 45 degrees away from the center of the auditorium. Anything more and a high percentage of the sound will be lost to useless areas of the stage. Unless you enforce this in the early choral rehearsals, you will be taking valuable time during the dress rehearsals. An illustration of this problem is in Leonard Bernstein's *West Side Story*. In the Quintet where three soloists, Tony, Maria, and Anita, are singing (usually with microphones), the pit orchestra is playing and the two gangs, the Jets and the Sharks, are singing on opposite sides of the stage. Since there are normally only ten or 12 in each gang, the problem of projection is critical. The vocal line is quite low in the singers' ranges, which compounds the felony still further. The only salvation is to accent the consonants until they are literally spit out at the audience. Have them speak only the consonants of the words so they do not overlook any. The endings of words are particularly vulnerable.

As much as possible, hold the early choral rehearsals on the stage where the play will eventually be presented. The stage is usually much less lively than the rehearsal hall, and the singers need to get used to the "feel" of the sound. Move the singers to different parts of the stage so they won't get in the habit of hearing only one type of choral sound. Any time you are rehearsing, have one or two singers sit out in the auditorium so they can appreciate the problems you are trying to overcome.

CHAPTER 11

Rehearsing Chamber Choirs and Festival Choruses

J ust as the style of the music often demands a certain size of chorus for proper realization, so does the size of the chorus often demand different rehearsal techniques. There are various reasons for this phenomenon. On the high school level, the chamber choir is usually a more select group with a higher degree of musical ability. Thus they will need less time to learn a given piece of music. The large chorus, on the other hand, may be a catch-all group which will require more detailed work and more note-picking.

Each director has his own ideal chorus size. Anything smaller than this ideal is a chamber choir and anything larger is a festival chorus (there is no common terminology for this type of chorus, so we will use the term festival chorus). For the purposes of this chapter, I have chosen an arbitrary size for each group. Most high school chamber choirs have from 12 to 20 voices with an equal number of singers on each part. The festival chorus is anything over 100 voices.

The Chamber Choir

These groups go by several titles—chamber singers, chamber choir, madrigal singers, and so forth. The size ranges from a soloist on each part to four or five singers in each section. This means from five to 20 singers in the average high school chamber choir. As was mentioned above, these singers will usually be selected from a larger chorus. This means that not as much time will be required to teach notes, less time will be required to get correct pronunciation, and fewer intonation problems will occur in music of equal difficulty. If you decide to use more difficult music, the time factor will go back up.

An accompanist is as necessary to a small group as to a large one. In addition to picking out notes, the accompanist may be called on to be the co-artist with a soloist or to play in a chamber ensemble with a few other instrumentalists. Also, some acquaintance with the organ and harpsichord is helpful if you are fortunate enough to have access to these instruments. More subtleties are involved in chamber music than in merely accompanying a rehearsal, so choose your accompanist very carefully.

The music chosen for a chamber choir should include several pieces for solo, duet, or trio to give some textural variety. A choir has a monotone sound since the voices can go neither as high nor as low, nor can they blow as loudly as instruments. An hour of choral singing can be horribly monotonous. This problem is compounded when the chorus is small and incapable of strong, dynamic accents. The insertion into the program of solo material of the same style as the choral music is a welcome relief to the audience. Obviously these solos need not be practiced during the regular rehearsal, although they might be sung once to illustrate to the other singers a new aspect of the music they, themselves, are singing. If an all-Renaissance program is in rehearsal, you should alternate pieces by the full chorus with pieces for three, four, or five soloists, or even the insertion of some instrumentally accompanied solos.

When you decide to use a few soloists, divide your group so that two or three different combinations of voices can work at the same time. This takes some preplanning, and without a doubt all singers will not be singing at all times, but you can work on two or three pieces in the same span of time you would be working on a single piece with the full chorus. Since only an accompanist and four or five singers are involved, you will not have to have large rooms for the groups which leave the general rehearsal for ensemble rehearsal. As the director you may choose to work only with one group for the full time, or you may choose to spend a few minutes with each group.

If the rehearsal period is of a normal length of 50 or 55 minutes, you will find it best to divide the period about equally between full rehearsal and divided ensemble rehearsal. There is a limit to the time most high school students can direct themselves with efficiency. A variation of the split rehearsal is to have a full rehearsal for about 15 minutes, then go to ensemble rehearsal for 20 to 30 minutes, and then reassemble for the final ten minutes or so. During this last segment of time, each of the ensembles will perform for the rest of the group. This gives them some incentive to get some good work done.

This emphasis on solo singing should be kept in mind while choosing the singers in a chamber choir. This is due not only to the necessity of singing along but also to the need of engaging in some minor acting while presenting a solo or ensemble number. In a large chorus of 60 or more, there is little facial expression the singers can use beyond a slight smile or a pleasant countenance. In a chamber group, there is greater opportunity for the singers to become individuals, even when singing as a group. The music chosen can be more personal and the singers will be much closer to the audience geographically. Facial expressions can be much more subtle but they must also be used more often than in a large group. This means the rehearsal time must include some instructions on personality and emotional projection by the singers. The singers may wish to recede into the bland, big-chorus appearance. If this happens, have them give a choral reading of the words (without pitch or rhythm) using extreme pronunciation and interpretative effects. This gets them off dead center and shows them the capabilities of the words. If this does not do enough to loosen them up, have them hum the notes and try to mirror the words in their faces. When they have both an understanding of the words and proper facial control, they should have a good stage appearance. A program by a chamber choir should be a stage event rather than simply a concert of choral music.

Allied with this acting requirement is a chance for more natural pronunciation. Final consonants will still be a problem but vowel changes and pronunciation can be more on the level of the spoken language. This does *not* mean using a regional dialect so beware of saying "sing it as you would speak it."

This naturalness of pronunciation should carry over into the physical appearance of the entire group. While bobbing and weaving has no place on a concert stage, certain postures, facial expressions, and bodily attitudes can effectively mirror the text. There is also the need for the soloist or soloists to move from within the group to a position nearer one another or closer to the piano. This takes rehearsal time. Just telling the singer "At this point in the concert you walk to the piano," is not sufficient for most high school singers. They need to experience some of the problems of walking from point A to point B while people watch.

Because there are fewer singers in a chamber choir, you will find your conductorial attitude to be one of close cooperation with individuals, rather than the more impersonal director/lecturer relationship when conducting a chorus of 100 singers. Your vocabulary may be modified slightly, in that you will not be quite as much of a cheerleader with the smaller group. Your directing gestures may be smaller.

You may decide that you, as a beat-giving director, will not be needed at all. More and more chamber choirs are performing without a director. One of the singers gives the pitch and a downbeat, and from that point their training takes over. This has some built-in hazards, in that left to their own devices like this you may hear your singers mess up an entrance or slowly approach total disintegration. These problems are more than outweighed, however, by the choir's rapid growth in confidence and poise when they realize they are totally responsible for the musical concert.

The rehearsal for this type of program must be a gradual receding of the conductor into the background. You train your singers to rely on the music in their minds and on the printed page, which means they will seldom perform without music in their hands. Some of the rehearsal time will be spent writing cryptic notes on the music such as "look up more often," "quick entrance after page turn," or "gradual ritardando." Even those dynamic or articulation markings already printed on the page may need to be repeated in bold strokes so they will be seen readily, at a glance. The music is not there to be read; it is for reference. Most singers need something to do with their hands during most concerts other than merely allowing them to dangle at their sides, and the music takes care of this problem. More importantly, the singers need an occasional jog of the memory. If they can get the first note and word they will probably do well, but if they are worrying about the first note they will probably not give much life to any part of the phrase. In addition to providing musical help, the printed page gives singers something to look at besides the audience. During rehearsal place some chairs in front of the singers to represent an audience, and have them practice looking at this substitute audience as often as possible. It takes some acting ability and they will feel rather foolish the first few times. If you choose not to direct the group, you will eventually become part of this "audience" as you move farther and farther back from the singers.

Some directors prefer to go halfway with the no-director gambit, by singing as part of the chorus but not standing in front of the group. I found this to be a handy performance method because I could give pitches and the starting downbeat, but I was still on hand in case something went awry. If an entrance was missed or the piece fell apart, it was my assumption that I could get things started again with less fuss and embarrassment than could a student director. Also, I could give discreet conducting gestures if such seemed to be called for. The singers were instructed to look at the audience about half of the time, the rest of the time being split between the music and the director. Eye contact with the audience is one of the great advantages a chamber choir has over a larger group, but this must be explained to the singers and practiced during the rehearsal period.

The Festival Chorus

What has been said concerning the chamber choir should in no way be deemed a slap at larger choruses of 100 voices or more.

Each chorus of different size can perform certain pieces of music which cannot be fully realized by the other, each has certain abilities the other does not have. The large chorus has as its most obvious attributes a richer and more voluptuous sound, as well as greater dynamic contrasts. A large work such as Brahms' *German Requiem* or Mendelssohn's *Elijah* would be unthinkable with a small chorus of 20 voices, no matter how mature and resonant. A delicate madrigal by Gesualdo or Morley would be trampled to death by 100 voices. Choose the music properly and many of your rehearsal problems will be solved automatically.

The rehearsal problems of a festival chorus are about the same as those for a "normal-sized" group of 50 to 60 singers. Part rehearsals will be about the same style, sight-reading will be approximately alike, and problems of intonation will be similar. Where you will find most of your problems will be in pronunciation, articulation, and rhythmic exactness. As a group gets larger it must spread out, so that a greater time span is used for the sound to get from one side of the chorus to the other. Although this may seem to be an infinitesimal unit of time, it is enough to mix and blur the sounds and cause an echo which will cut across brief rests.

One of the plus factors of having 25 or 35 sopranos instead of five or ten, is that your job of blending is taken care of automatically. You may have five or six ghastly voices, but when they are averaged into the larger group they lose their individually outstanding characteristics. This automatic blending may be a mixed blessing, because the sound has a monochrome patina to it which requires much work and rehearsal time to become an exciting and intense tone quality. As you spend less time on getting individual voices to blend, you will spend more time getting a true *pianissimo* or some modification of the basic bland tone. As with any other musical organization, merely singing in tune is not enough. There must also be music.

In a large chorus, you may have more of a problem in balancing sections than with a small, select chorus which has the same number of voices on each part. There will probably be more female voices, with the ratio sometimes as unbalanced as two girls to one boy. Rehearsal time must be scheduled to allow you time to try different seating arrangements. As was stated in another chapter, the front row of singers determines to a great extent the sound of your chorus. For this reason, the traditional plan of having the girls on the front rows and the boys on the back rows of the risers cuts farther into the available male sound. Having vertical sections allows each voice part to have a clear shot at the overall sound, thus eliminating much of your problem of balance between sections. If altos are added to the tenor line, have the girls stand behind the tenors so the alto sound is merely filler and the boys provide the basic tenor quality.

One problem of inaccurate articulation, or at least inaudibly correct articulation, is in the ♩. ♪ rhythm. The sixteenth note is often blended into the first note until all of the rhythmic vitality is lost. This can be helped by making the actual notation

♪ ⅞ ♪ . Because of the fullness of the tone of 100 singers, there will be no noticeable stopping of the sound, only a dip in the intensity before the next note is sung. It gives the sixteenth note a chance to begin a tone instead of being merely a continuation of a previous tone. A phrase such as Figure 11–1

Figure 11–1

has very little intensity or rhythmic drive when compared with Figure 11–2.

Figure 11–2

A secondary problem connected with this lack of rhythmic definition is that the chorus will gradually lose speed as the con-

149

sonants are pronounced less and less exactly. The singers must realize that the consonants must always come a tiny space of time before the beat so that the vowel *begins* on the beat. In rapid scale passages this is a difficult thing to master, but master it they must if they are to keep the rhythmic vitality and tempo up to the proper level. Try having them speak only the consonants of a phrase, then sing only the vowels, and finally both together. Singing only the vowels will give them a feeling for the correct tempo, and speaking only the vowels will uncover some sounds they may have missed. The use of a metronome is sometimes necessary to prove to the singers that they are singing behind the beat.

The singers must be warned that they will hear a much choppier sound than will the audience. They will hear themselves and will possibly wonder at such a technique. Explain that the sound as perceived by the audience is the proper sound, not the sound of the individual singer.

There are certain psychological changes in going from a small or medium-sized chorus to a large chorus. The larger the chorus, the more these changes are magnified. In very large choruses of 200 or 300 singers, you may very well turn into a cheerleader with large, ungainly gestures and a large, ungainly sound. The gestures need not become extremely large, but a slightly larger pattern may be in order at times. This suggestion for a slightly larger beat is given because the larger chorus may be made up of less experienced singers who need more obvious gestures than a chorus of experienced singers.

It will take a considerable amount of time to get the first true *pianissimo*. The singers will be making almost no sound at all and they may feel cheated. Explain to them that on the *fortissimo* passages you intend to let the billows roar, but on the softest parts you intend to fulfill the musical requirements. There is a peculiar mob psychology in directing the festival chorus. It is a much more impersonal group than a chamber choir. The individual must submerge his identity into the section of 20 or 30 or 40 singers. Eye contact, in both rehearsal and concert, between the director and each individual singer is helpful in giving the singer more of a feeling of importance.

A large group also has a much greater problem of pronunciation than has a small group. The cross-echo from one end of the risers to the other can blur almost any word. *Ss* and *zz*, on the other hand, have a habit of being too prominent. To keep these sibilants from dominating the choral fabric, you may have to resort to a brief *diminuendo* just before the sibilant, as in Figure 11–3.

THI   SS   I - ZZMM AH - EE   LAND
THIS   IS   MY   LAND

Figure 11–3

This is a time-consuming rehearsal problem. In *forte* and *fortissimo* passages there will be no great problem; this occurs only in dynamic levels of *mezzo-piano* and below.

Large festival choruses, as often as not, perform extended works rather than short three- or four-minute pieces. This usually means a concert performance using music scores rather than a memorized performance. For this reason also, you may need to use larger gestures than you would with a smaller choir which has memorized its music. The problems of rehearsing the large work will be covered more fully in Chapter 13.

CHAPTER 12

Rehearsing the
All-Male and
All-Female Choir

The problems of rehearsing an all-male or an all-female choir on the high school level fall under two basic classifications: physical and psychological. Attitudes toward themselves, their relative ages, the age span within the chorus, and the community acceptance of singing as a legitimate enterprise all impinge upon the psychological problems of the high school singer. The physical problems, on the other hand, are summed up in one phrase: can the singers hear and reach the notes?

The All-Male Choir

These choruses often use the title Glee Club or some other name to disguise the fact that they are in fact a choir. Some Americans have an ingrained aversion to singing by men. Singing is considered to be women's work and beneath notice by real men. This attitude directly affects the work you will be doing in your rehearsal, since you will need to choose music to fit the singers' psychological needs and also music which will break down the image that "singing is sissyish." As your program builds and former members of a men's chorus return, there will be less of a problem. However, for at least the first year or two, your problems may turn out to be more psychological than physical.

To go beyond the scope of this book for just a paragraph, I heartily recommend two-part and three-part music for beginning male choruses, even those that happen to have enough high tenors and low basses to make a decent sound. By cutting down on the number of parts, you both cut down on the rehearsal time involved in learning notes and you make each section proportionally larger. This gives more confidence to unlettered voices. There are dozens of fine works, both accompanied and unaccompanied and in two-part or three-part settings for male voices.

As with any other chorus, a certain amount of time in every rehearsal must be given to sight-reading and ear-training. High school boys have the immense problem of having their musical instrument (the body frame) in a constant but disproportionate state of growth. Clarinettists would have considerably more trouble learning to play their instruments if one month the barrel grew an inch longer and the next month the keys all grew thicker. This growth causes some lack of vocal control among ninth- and tenth-grade students, and to some degree through the senior year. Only by constantly working during the rehearsal time to keep the ear keenly in tune, will the singers be able to sing properly throughout the year. Due to this physical growth, the warm-up period must be emphasized more with the boys' chorus than with the girls' chorus. Your inventive genius will be taxed to its fullest in keeping interest through a three-minute warm-up, to say nothing of getting the boys (including both basses and tenors) to learn the technique of singing with the head tone and in falsetto.

It is best not to program some familiar piece for the first few weeks of rehearsal. Inexperienced singers head for the most familiar line of music, regardless of whether it is their own music or not. Keep your choice of music simple, keep it exciting, and keep it unfamiliar. Popular music is a poor choice unless you find a particularly good work in a two-part arrangement with sufficient musical and textual interest to keep them occupied for several rehearsals. Most popular arrangements for male voices are drearily homophonic and uninteresting. Without a doubt your singers will ask for some popular work which they happen to have on a recording by a popular group, usually with guitars and powerful amplification. DON'T!! The disappointment is too great when the boys compare their own efforts with the recorded piece.

Because a rehearsal of a group of high school boys is often on the verge of breaking into laughter or talking or some other disaster, you must be ready at any instant to go to another piece of music for a change of pace. Never give them any time to start talking or you will have lost the rehearsal. For this reason, some techniques work very well for girls or for mixed choruses but they fail with a boys' chorus. The split rehearsal where one-half of the chorus sings while the other half listens will work, if the competitive spirit is high enough to make each half want to outdo the other. There is the ever-present problem that the nonsinging half will heckle the singing half. As the singers mature and as some group pride is built, this will be less of a problem.

When a solo voice is needed, it may be best to have the entire section or even the entire choir learn the solo; then have the individual voices, in turn, sing the solo when it comes due. Younger singers often have more enthusiasm than good judgment, so take advantage of this fact and let them get some confidence in solo singing during the rehearsal period. In the majority of high schools, the boys' chorus has the better voices lifted out for performance in the main chorus so few top-notch voices are in the boys' group for very long. Thus your rehearsals with the boys' group takes on greater importance since they will probably be performing less. Try the solos with two or three voices if you have some relatively shy boys who would cringe at the thought of performing alone.

The physical problems of reaching the pitches, whether up or down, is the most obvious problem for the high school boys' chorus. Warm-up exercises and vocalises are the only answer. You will need to modify the music they are singing to make the pieces into exercises, for developing the individual voices. As the chorus learns the music, have them sing each piece on several neutral vowels and sing staccato notes with proper breathing and posture. The staccato notes force them to sing on the exact notes without scooping into the pitches or adjusting the pitch after they begin the tone. For sight-reading practice on tonal music have the entire chorus read each line, unless it is too low for them to reach, in which case the ones with problems can sing it an octave high. For the high notes, have the entire group sing in head tone or falsetto.

Be very sparing of choral works which force the tenors to go above the staff very often. This is another reason for using Tenor/Bass and Tenor/Baritone/Bass (TB and TBB) arrangements. In these voicings, the high tenor is usually eliminated and the tenor line goes to about an F but seldom above. It is extremely helpful if the accompanist can transpose both up and down, so that the tenors can sing lower and the basses higher when practicing tough passages. Also, the accompanist should understand about playing an octave higher when merely duplicating the parts. For some reason, this technique does not work as well when accompanying the full group as when playing only one or two lines.

The beginning boys' chorus will usually stick with tonal music, at least for the first few weeks or months. Getting the singers to listen for other pitches for tuning can be a slow process. One technique is to eliminate all pitches but one. All this requires is for one part to sing while another part sings a single pedal tone on either the tonic or dominant, preferably the latter. This gives the section singing the music some nonchanging tone to relate to, and it gives the second section practice in holding a long tone on a nonchanging pitch. This is not an easy task for a beginning singer, so do not consider it as marking time for the dominant holder. There will be some pitches which will sound somewhat dissonant and may cause the singers to frown at the clash between, say, an F-sharp and a G if both are held for some time. This has an added benefit of giving a slightly tart flavor to an otherwise bland piece, thus stretching both the ears and the taste of the singers.

The "changing voice" (sometimes called cambiata) is in a class all its own. There are techniques of training this midway voice which are specialized and involve more details than can be handily covered in this book. Also, it is basically a junior high voice and is seldom encountered in the high school choral class. If it does happen to appear in your boys' chorus, you have the choice of putting him or them in the high tenor section, or if they cannot get down to the tenor notes, you may need to ask them to wait until the next semester to sign up. If you have an average boys' chorus of from 20 to 40 voices, you will probably not have the proper time to give to such a specialized voice in the classroom situation, and you certainly cannot choose all of your music to fit the changing voices. Do not worry about them missing chorus for a semester or even a year. Make them your recording engineer and librarian. They will certainly be ninth or tenth graders and will still have at least two years of singing ahead of them.

The All-Female Choir

The Girls' Chorus or Girls' Glee Club is, like the male counterpart, usually a training group for the first mixed chorus. There are certain differences which make it a better singing group, voice for voice, than the boys' chorus. The most obvious plus factor is the lack of the changing voice. The girls have been using virtually the same voice for several years by the time they get into high school; whereas, the boys will have been growing a new voice every few months during the junior high period. This stable vocal range of the girls may mature and deepen slightly with practice but the range will not extend greatly. Second, girls are a more malleable social group than boys, so the discipline problems are less acute. Finally, the higher voices are more easily tuned than the lower voices.

Because the girls' chorus is normally a training chorus, the top voices will not be in the group for very long. It will also not be concertizing as much as the main chorus, so the rehearsal period must be a more self-sufficient entity. The rehearsal period can be an end in itself if it is fast and enjoyable, which means no lost time and much obvious progress. Obvious, that is, to the singers.

The warm-up period should include sight-reading material, just as with the boys' chorus, except that you can work on more dissonant intervals more quickly because the voices will be better controlled. The warm-up segment of the rehearsal will not show as much obvious progress as with the boys' chorus because the girls' voices will already be on a higher level of accuracy and maturity. Also, boys' voices, even those in late adolescence, have more power than girls' voices of equivalent ages and thus can have a wider emotional range. The rehearsal for the girls' chorus should include exercises in modifying the tone quality from dark to light, from thick vibratos to straight tones, and from childlike timbres to mature sounds. This is necessary to show the singers the extent of their vocal possibilities. One of the most monotonous sounds in music is that of a chorus of high school female voices. Unless you choose the music carefully and use a variety of sounds in carefully prepared performances, you will have a bland treble sound with virtually no audience interest after the first two or three selections. The rehearsal is the time to get this variety of timbres; by concert time it is too late.

One vocal sound usually ignored in the high school chorus is the so-called "chest voice" or "chest register." An exercise for developing this range of the female voice is discussed at the end of Chapter 8. The problems with this sound are in its overuse with immature voices and in the director's allowing the sound to continue up into the normal voice range. It should be used briefly in the warm-up for several weeks until the girls, both altos and sopranos, can slide gently into the tone quality with little or no noticeable break from the regular voice. This should happen about middle C or the B-flat below. This voice can eventually be taken down to E-flat or occasionally below with considerably more volume and resonance than with the normal voice. The sopranos can also work on this range without affecting their upper range, but again you must beware of using it too much or too quickly with immature voices. When going from the chest voice upward into the regular voice, practice gradually changing from one to the other at about middle C or the D above. I recall one college student of mine who, as a college freshman, had a shattering break from the chest voice to the regular voice at the fourth line D! Her high school instructor had allowed her to use the loud, tenorish chest voice far beyond the point where she should have returned to her normal voice. Her voice was virtually ruined. Do not work on the chest register every rehearsal; every other rehearsal should suffice. Gradually the girls will begin experimenting with the sound and they will work it into their everyday repertory of techniques and sounds.

The suggestion concerning the use of two-part works for the beginning boys' chorus also applies to the girls' chorus. At first keep the music simple, exciting, and unfamiliar. Eventually you will want to try more experimental types of music with four, five, or more parts or with two or three divided choirs.

The rehearsal of a two-part work requires only that you teach them enough to find and follow their individual parts, and then separate them geographically so there is a minimum of sound drift between the two sections. This could mean placing yourself and the accompanist in the center of the room with the two sections on opposite sides of you and facing away from each other. This cuts the sound down appreciably, except for the reflected sound which has less definition. If this is not enough separation, have each section form a large circle facing inward so the sound goes into the center. It is obvious that the singers will not be watching your directing, so don't expect much in the way of subtleties since you will be directing by voice not by hand motion. Remember, this is an early rehearsal by a green chorus. Take one problem at a time and work on it with any technique you feel will show progress. As they improve, have half of each section form its own circle and perform the work while the other half listens. There is much less of a discipline problem with girls, so this device works readily.

A three-part work can be rehearsed in the same manner, forming three circles. In fact, this rehearsing in sections formed into circles works for any number of parts, with women, men, or mixed choruses. When the singers become strong enough as individual singers they will not need to move to these sections, and eventually they will be able to sight-read in a scrambled or integrated seating situation. When this ideal is reached, your rehearsals will be much more profitable from a measures-learned-per-rehearsal standpoint. They can watch you while singing instead of listening with half an ear for the piano.

If this seems to paint a bleak picture of the male chorus and the female chorus on the high school level, it is only because my years of directing such choruses taught me that September is a grim month from the standpoint of choral tone and ability. Fundamental abilities must be taught and developed or all the rest of the school year will be a succession of flat chords and mispronounced sentences. Usually the more inexperienced singers will be placed in these monochrome groups. Your job is to take them where they are and teach them the basics of choral singing while giving them enough musical excitement to keep them interested in learning. It is not an easy job, but it becomes considerably easier if your philosophy is one of progress and not simply one of performance. There are several fine books which give the standard patterns for conducting. These are necessary for well-trained vocal organizations. For the beginning choruses and choristers we must be more realistic. Accept the fact that they cannot appreciate or follow directorial niceties until they have enough ability to get beyond the Himalayan difficulties of developing the right pitches and rhythms.

CHAPTER 13

Working on One Extended Choral Piece

More and more high schools are making a practice of programming one large choral work for presentation during the year. This can range from the little *Mass in G* of Franz Schubert for a school assembly to presentations of the Fauré *Requiem* or a Webern Cantata with a full orchestra. The problems of instrumental and solo rehearsal have been covered in Chapter 10. This chapter is concerned with the problems of working on one piece by one composer for an extended number of rehearsals.

Although one style of music will remain with you throughout any extended work, this does not mean that only one texture will be used. If only one texture is available in a work of more than six or eight minutes, you may have chosen a poor work. Monotony will not be a great problem in rehearsing a work of 30 or 40 minutes, since you can choose sections within movements for contrast of textures and emotions. This problem of boredom when the singers spend an hour on the same type of music was discussed in Chapter 5, as was the problem of outlining the rehearsal from beginning to end. What was said then about keeping interest through a diversity of textures and tempos applies to the extended work as well as to a series of smaller works.

Memorizing or Reading

Virtually all performances of large choral works are given with the singers using the printed music scores; that is, with the music under control but not memorized. It was mentioned in the previous chapter, that when music is used in concert it is only for reference and not for actual reading. The singers must be trained to hold the music correctly so that it looks proper from the point of view of the audience and is adjusted so the singer can see at a glance the musical passage he needs. If the music is held too much on a vertical plane, the audience sees nothing but a lake of paper covers and music folders. If it is held too flat or too low the music may be difficult to read, and if it is too high it may muffle the sound. If the music is held according to personal whim, the whole chorus will look snaggle-toothed.

While some directors want the music held relatively far out in front of the singers, I have found that a comfortable position comes about when the singers have the right hand hold the music, the right elbow against the hip bone, the music at right angles to a line from the eyes and somewhat above the waist, and the left hand doing all of the page turning. This may seem overly complicated in the telling, but the actual practice of it is quite simple. While standing on risers you will need more room between singers for the scores so held, so be sure to practice occasionally on the risers so the singers can become used to this space (or lack of space).

The ideal situation is to have the music virtually memorized. It is too easy for the singers to be lulled into a false security when they know the music will be available during the concert. To force the singers to think ahead after the music is mostly learned, instead of relying entirely on the printed score, have half of each section close the music and perform from memory. There will be some bobbling and mumbling of words but there will also be some memory stretching. The obvious next step is to let the other half of the chorus try its wings on the same passage. Much music can be learned even when the musician is not singing.

The technique of rehearsing in reverse is highly recommended for the extended work as well as the memorized short piece, and for the same reasons. All too often the best-known section is the first section, and all succeeding parts are less well known. The singers are constantly going toward music which is less under control. This keeps the singers a bit on edge. If a movement of a work has four sections, in the later rehearsals work on section four, then on three and four together, then on two, three, and four, and finally do the entire movement from the beginning.

This plan of working from the back to the front also applies to the full work. You will be picking and choosing movements to rehearse according to the difficulty and the state of preparedness of each, but you must also judge carefully so that the last movements are not given less attention than the first.

Soloists and Instrumentalists

Most extended works employ both soloists and instrumentalists other than the regular accompanist. Chapter 10 covers these "nonchoral" rehearsals. If an outside soloist is going to be brought in for the concert, you will need to assign solos which occur within choral sections to members of the chorus so the overall musical fabric can be understood by the singers. These solos can be rotated among several people, thus giving some modest solo practice to those who would not normally be singing in public.

You will need to match the solo voices both to the choir and to each other as much as possible. Some voices may be individually beautiful but a brilliant tenor, a growling bass, a flutelike soprano, and a brassy contralto will be a bit difficult to work into a decent solo ensemble. There is also the style problem of blindingly rich soloists alternating with an immature high school choral sound. You will need to explain this problem to both the soloists and the choir. During your rehearsals, you can make some adjustments in tone quality so that everyone tries to find a middle ground.

If the work you are rehearsing will eventually use an orchestra for the concert, you need to allow the singers to sing louder than if the concert would use only a piano for the accompaniment.

An orchestra is considerably louder and will cover up a lot of the choral sound, particularly lackadaisical consonants. It is more work and requires more rehearsal time to balance the individual parts, since you cannot rely on your ears alone. You must figure out which instruments are going to be playing at a given time and make your volume adjustments accordingly. The chorus will respond differently if the strings are playing *pizzicato* for the accompaniment than if the entire wind section is blazing away. *Forte* is relevant, depending on the number of singers, the number of instrumentalists, and the size of the hall.

The tone quality you ask for in rehearsal is also dependent to a certain extent on the instruments which are playing. You must decide whether the composer wanted the voices to contrast or blend with the instruments. There is no way to say for sure what the composer's intent was without consulting specific musical scores, but you can at least come close to telling what the composer wanted by seeing if the instruments play the same notes and rhythms as the singers, or if the instruments are playing separate melodic lines and more or less distinct rhythms. If the instruments are merely doubling the voices, it is probably best to try to match and blend with the instrumental tone. The familiar *Ave Verum Corpus* by W. A. Mozart (Figure 13–1) has this type of writing.

A contrasting accompaniment would be illustrated by the opening chorus of J. S. Bach's Cantata No. 140, *Wachet Auf*, which is shown in Figure 13–2 (page 166).

Here there is no definite tone quality called for, there are no doublings by instruments with the vocal lines, so you are left to your own choices as to the tone qualities for the vocal parts. The term "tone qualities" is used because this particular work has different textures on the soprano line with its *cantus firmus* and the other three voices which form an accompaniment (see the final chapter of this book for an extensive rehearsal analysis of this choral section).

This same problem of blending or contrasting the vocal and instrumental timbres exists when you rehearse with a piano but plan a concert with an organ. You must determine the organ registration while the choir is still in rehearsal. If a bland mixture of strings and flutes is to be used there will be little trouble making

W. A. Mozart, "Ave Verum Corpus"

Figure 13-1

your high school choir heard. If, however, the organist is of the Romantic Magnificence school of organ playing, where every chord is a triumph of resonance, you will have to work with both the organist and the choir to find that musical middle ground mentioned before. Use the music as the point of departure and determine your volumes and timbres early enough in the rehearsal schedule so the choir can become used to the sound. You cannot spring it on the singers at the last rehearsal and expect much of a result.

Warn your singers as they are rehearsing with the piano, that the first rehearsal with the orchestra may bring up some problems

J. S. Bach "Cantata No. 140"

Figure 13–2

in finding their entering pitches. The piano reduction does not always play the orchestral pitches in the same octave, and in some instances does not even play all of the pitches. If the singers get used to rehearsing with specific pitches played by a percussive piano, they may lose their bearings when that particular pitch does not appear at a given time. Also, the piano is a percussion instrument which means a more accented tone. Sometimes it is easier to find the pitch of a piano playing the E above middle C *pianissimo* than a flute playing the same level and pitch. As a director, you should be aware of these problems when combining the instruments with the chorus for the first time. If they bobble an entrance because the timbre or volume was not what they had been expecting, you do not need to make a big scene about it since you know they will probably get it the next time. Know your instrumental score and piano reduction so you can warn the chorus of these problems before the instrumental rehearsal.

The Language Barrier

It is the common practice today to perform in Latin whatever was originally written in Latin and to translate other languages into English, with the exception of a few sacrosanct German works such as Brahms' *German Requiem*. This is not the place to discuss the merits of original languages vs. translations. Most Latin works are now coming off the presses with English translations, so "you pay your money and take your pick."

If you opt for Latin, it is best for a beginning chorus to stick to a relatively familiar text such as the Mass, the Requiem, the Te Deum, or a similarly common text for the first foreign-language work. Pronunciation will not be a large problem but it will take rehearsal time to begin with. Before you begin rehearsal, be sure that the pronunciation of each word of the Latin text is pencilled in the score. You should use a standard pronunciation guide for this and not try to rely completely on your memory, at least not at first. There are two standard pronunciations of Latin, the Classical and that of the Roman Catholic Church. The difference is basically that the first (Classical) uses more diphthong sounds while the Roman pronunciation is virtually without diphthong sounds. There are also a few slight consonant differences. By and large the choral world has chosen the Roman pronunciation. The Classical Latin sounds are quite a bit like the pronunciation of certain sounds in Italian, while the Roman pronunciation is more austere and reserved. This austerity fits the character of much of the choral music you will be performing, but certainly not all of it. Allow some time during the first rehearsal for explaining the pronunciation to your choir. Also allow some time to explain to the students taking a Latin course in your school that your pronunciation differs from that of their teacher.

167

CHAPTER 14

Meeting the
Problems of
Contemporary
Music

One of the biggest problems in rehearsing contemporary choral music is "Where do I start?" If the piece is extremely dissonant, has an obscure text, awkward melodic intervals, and frequent meter changes, you will either drop the entire piece or you may incorrectly try to work everything out at one time. The rehearsal of a contemporary musical work is a logical succession of understanding and conquering the problems as set up by the composer.

The first stage is to assume that the composer and the publisher (if the piece is not in manuscript form) have some faith in the work as an artistic entity. In my years of writing and performing contemporary choral works, I have met only one composer who attempted to write show-off music. The rest have without exception been people who wished to communicate their own particular vision of the Muse. They have been more or less successful according to their talents and their clear or blurred vision, but they were

169

all writing honest music. If you cannot believe in each piece of music you try, you will probably wind up with a caricature of the composer's intentions. You will also communicate this disbelief to your singers.

The second step is to analyze the text to see if you can identify with the words, and further, to see if the text is used by the composer for its primary purpose of communicating a literary idea or as a source for musical sounds. This determination is necessary or you will spend useless time in rehearsal trying to get a clearly understood text when the composer couldn't care less whether the words are understandable or not. In the event that the composer is only trying to get sounds for musical development, you may decide that the text is the last thing which needs work. The text may even be nonsense with little relation to the singers, ancient examples being the *fa-la-la* refrains and other nonsense syllables of Renaissance madrigals and ballads. These would require less concern with pronunciation than would a setting of a lyrical narrative poem, although the attention to tone quality would be just as critical.

The third step is to determine whether the primary concern is with individual melodies as complete entities or whether the most obvious element should be the sequence of chords. Of course there will probably be both kinds of musical writing in a piece of even modest length, but you must determine where the emphasis is at a given time. When you have determined where the interest lies at a particular spot, you will know how to divide your rehearsal time and also you will know when a section is clear enough to fulfill its musical function. Worrying about the harmonic structure too much may make the melodic line of each voice part stilted, angular, and uninteresting if the interest is primarily horizontal.

The fourth step is to emphasize the articulation and dynamic markings on the score so you can see what the sound texture is going to be. Contemporary music, particularly the experimental music, is highly concerned with the texture of the sounds, meaning the accents, sudden dynamic changes, nonword sounds such as whistles, sighs, clicks, and finger snaps, as well as peculiar tone qualities and word fragmentations. To attempt a blended sound similar to that used on a Brahms motet when a jagged nasal sound

170

is called for, is to totally mishandle the composer's work. It is as bad in its own sphere as singing flat is in the realm of intonation.

Finally, list the elements which need to be learned in the order in which they may be most easily assimilated. These elements are: (1) melody, (2) harmony or the proper intonation of various lines of music, (3) articulation, and (4) the text and its meaning. This is only a list of the elements in a musical work, and does not mean that this is the order of importance for rehearsing each choral work. With traditional tonal music, the most common approach is to begin rehearsing the pitches. This may or may not be the right angle of attack with your piece of contemporary music. For instance, in some pieces which have intricate rhythmic structures but relatively simple pitches, the correct thing to do is polish up the rhythmic problems, then make sure the articulation is correct because these two elements usually go hand in hand. When doing this you can put each part on a different pitch, so the singers will be able to tell which part is theirs. Another method is to separate the sections around the rehearsal room so there is less interference between sections.

Usually the singers wish to know what they are singing about, so an explanation of the imagery in the text will probably be necessary. This may be some of the toughest explaining you will ever run into, but don't underestimate the ability of high school students to comprehend complicated texts. Your problem is how much to feed them and where in the rehearsal schedule they should be fed.

If the music is linear and quite dissonant, you may choose to begin with part rehearsals, and these would occur before any type of complete run-through is attempted. The reason for this procedure is that all of the lines combined may give a false impression of the difficulty; whereas, learning the lines singly and then in duets will gradually introduce them to the sound of the work without drowning them in the noise of the full piece. The part rehearsals need not be long. Ten or 15 minutes each for three or four different rehearsals should take care of the main problems for any three-minute work of medium difficulty.

Some pieces of difficult music may seem to be impossible to perform with your present chorus, when in reality all they need is more maturity and exposure to similar music. I recall one very fine high school chorus which had so much difficulty with Kodály's *Jesus and the Traders* after rehearsing it during September and October, that the director withdrew it in disgust. Fortunately, parts of the music which had been conquered by the students remained in the back of their minds. In March they asked to be allowed to try again. This time they had the technique and confidence to give an excellent performance. A word of caution: *unless the singers have the ability to sing a tune without getting off, they will be unable to sing this (or any other) music.* Sight-reading, ear-training, and a gradual introduction to the vocabulary of contemporary sounds are necessary before the singers will accept such works.

When working with part rehearsals, keep the sections separate until they can get through the music without the help of the piano. Until they can sing without this extra help, they do not truly know the music. As soon as this goal of unaccompanied singing is met, have two parts sing the music—with the accompanist if necessary. If possible, use different combinations of voices in the two-section rehearsal. In other words, have each section sing with each other section in two-part rehearsal before putting them together as a full unit. The indicator of when to progress to the addition of more sections is when the two sections can perform the whole piece without the piano. In highly dissonant choral music, beware of putting the whole work together too soon. Be sure to check Chapter 9 for some suggestions concerning the part rehearsal.

Much contemporary choral music, meaning that music which is truly contemporary and not merely warmed-over, nineteenth-century schmaltz, utilizes intricate interval relationships as an integral part of the vocabulary. Since these intervals are such a prominent part of the choral writing, your job is to get as pure a set of intervals as possible. This may require adjusting the tone quality so the intervals stand out in more stark relief. With most music up to 1900 the intervals were not as critical. They had to be in tune, but they were not to be displayed as items of isolated and emphasized music. In music with highly dissonant chords and intervals, the rehearsal must be arranged so these intervals are learned precisely until they "ring." Only then will they be obvious enough to both the audience and the singers so they fulfill the composer's intentions.

The tuning of intervals is not the problem often supposed. The first thing to be done in the rehearsal is to work with the various sections on tuning perfect fourths, fifths, and octaves. These must be locked in to perfect intonation so solidly that the overtones are readily heard—the "ring" mentioned in the previous paragraph. Without the knowledge of what a perfect interval sounds like, it will be almost impossible to tune up some of the complex chords of contemporary music. Make up sight-reading sheets which consist of only two-part melodies moving in a succession of perfect fourths, fifths, and octaves, as in Figure 14–1.

Figure 14–1

Then have the singers sing these exercises in compound intervals, giving the exercises an organum sound.

Figure 14–2

The stark, uncompromising sound is necessary before the singers will begin listening for these intervals disguised in seventh, ninth, or eleventh chords, in chords built on fourths instead of thirds, or in the completely atonal works. When their ears are tuned to these open sounds, you can proceed to the actual music. As you put the music together, look for these perfect intervals between voices and tune them first. This will keep the pitch from sagging and give the singers something more easily tuned than, say, a major seventh or minor ninth.

Until the singers acknowledge in their own minds that such music is actually singable, they will balk at even attempting such difficult pieces. Chapter 6 has some suggestions for sight-reading material which will gradually introduce more and more dissonant material into their choral vocabulary. Once the ice has been broken, the students will take to this type of music as if they were born to it. Only two necessities exist: (1) you must treat this music throughout every rehearsal as if it were the most natural musical language imaginable; and (2) the sight-reading and concert material must be introduced to them in a logical sequence, so they are never completely submerged in unfamiliar music. This is, of course, assuming the singers can sing relatively jagged vocal lines.

If you determine that the articulation elements, meaning the accents and "spice" elements, are among the most important parts of the choral work, you may need to isolate these and work on them alone. Works which use choral speaking should have the spoken and sung parts separated and learned individually before putting them together. The reason for this is in the lack of rhythmic definition given the spoken word by high school choruses. If the rhythm of the spoken text is given exactly and not merely chanted, you will need to rehearse this as much as if there was a melody with the rhythm. Your first job will be to list the number of different devices the composer has used to see how they differ from one another. Do not mistake a staccato marking for a slight accent. A *subito piano* marking is not a gradual diminuendo. This pertains to all choral music, of course, but in contemporary music the changes are often more abrupt and occur more frequently. The composer may be writing music which was inspired by and simulates electronic music, and unless you understand this point and are ready to fulfill the composer's intentions, you will not have a completely successful rehearsal or concert.

The tone qualities demanded by contemporary choral works will make high demands on your rehearsal technique. The American "bland" sound will not be enough. An ultra-straight tone takes time to explain and develop so that the singers do not tighten up the wrong muscles. A rich, dark tone may be called for immediately after a flutelike tone, or the men may be chanting with a masculine and growling voice while the women are singing with an almost electronic sound. Your vocabulary of rehearsal phrases will get its greatest tests directing contemporary music, since you will need to give brief but accurate instructions almost continually.

Contemporary music often draws these extremes in tone color and articulation within the space of a few measures. It is one thing to be able to follow a Morley madrigal with a Bruckner motet and a quite different thing to make this drastic a switch within the space of a measure. In the first instance, you will have time between the two works to shift your style gears and prepare yourself and the choir for the differences in emotions and timbre. In the second instance, the choir may be required to change in the space of a breath. Far from disliking this the singers will find, if they are average high school students, that such changes are exhilarating.

Contemporary music is no more difficult to rehearse than traditional tonal music; it only requires a specialized preparation and a logical rehearsal schedule. It may take a bit more time to rehearse per concert minute, but this is not always the case. Most of the rehearsal suggestions given in earlier chapters will work with contemporary music, such as playing in a different octave when accompanying individual vocal lines, rehearsing in reverse, forming circles within each section, and so on. The problem is to take the piece apart until all of the components are clearly visible; then make a preference list so you will know which parts to work on first; and finally put the piece back together. This is also the theory of all rehearsals, except that some music may be rehearsed so that two or three elements are worked on at the same time, such as in a Bach chorale setting. Here the rhythm is seldom a problem, the melodies cause only a minimal amount of trouble, and the text (unless in another language) is obvious. After the first time through such a setting you will be polishing.

It has been emphasized that only one thing should be worked on at a time. This does not mean that anything else that is possible from a performance standpoint should be deliberately ignored, only that the focus should be on one element and whatever else can be attained is gravy. A passage that is written *pianissimo* might be sung *mezzo-piano* without harming the work, and you could get this with one or two mentionings. They should not sing *forte* on such a passage, unless you have a specific reason for it. Get them as close to the eventual dynamic level as you can without making a big event out of it, unless you are working primarily on dynamics.

CHAPTER 15

Judging When a Choral Work Is Ready for Performance

Each piece of music that is rehearsed (as opposed to the music which is merely sight-read for practice) is presumed to be headed for a concert or program. Among the larger problems of a conductor, is the requirement that he so structure the rehearsals that a piece of music emerges from the final rehearsals ready for the concert, neither overworked nor under-rehearsed. The various stages in the preparation of a work—the first reading, the learning of difficult passages, and the final polishing—must follow in a proper sequence aimed at the concert.

There are two levels of preparation, the psychological and the physical. If the singers believe in themselves and trust you, they are psychologically ready. If they can hit the notes and sustain them in tune they are physically ready. Just how you determine when these two states exist is your last problem before the concert.

177

The More They Can Do for Themselves, the Better Prepared They Are

Even on a concert which you plan to direct, it is a useful idea to turn the singers loose without a director and see how well they follow the directions you have given them. If the dynamics are noticeably better, if the cutoffs are clean and the pronunciation crisp, then they are in good shape. It may be that you have unknowingly gone farther with the rehearsals on some passages than is good for the choir. Each singing group has a point at which everything that is learned seems to push out something else. Giving them their head is one way of learning what is ready and what may never be ready for the program. If there are some intricate cutoffs or entrances, you may choose to let a student director do the directing.

How Much from Memory?

If you are planning to use music on the concert, one way to test the singers for preparedness is to have them fold their music and sing from memory. The accompanist can keep on playing so the music will not break down completely. There may be a lot of humming on places where the text is not known and some entrances will be mumbled. As the director, you have to determine their level of preparation from this test. Another method is to have half of them sing from memory while the other half uses music. If they are able to pick up the phrases after the first word or two, they are in relatively good shape. If they cannot carry through with even a simple melody, then they may be psychologically unprepared. If they do not think they can do it, they probably will "botch it up."

Reposition the Sections

Near the end of the rehearsal of a work, reposition the various sections so that a new sound comes to the singers' ears. If you are using vertical sections, move them around so that the sections are in horizontal rows. Then alternate rows which are in the front so you can hear clearly which section is having trouble.

Sing Standing in Quartets on the Risers

This is a version of the scrambled or integrated seating plan (see Chapter 5). The goal is to isolate each voice and see if stark terror appears on any face. Slightly inaccurate singing should be no cause for alarm, but if there is a general lack of definition to the attacks and the pronunciation is slipshod, then you probably have a lot of work to do before your singers are ready for the performance. This is, of course, dependent upon the relative maturity and experience of the chorus. The reasoning behind the use of this technique is that if they cannot perform the piece with the sections mixed up, there may be too many "leaners" in the sections.

Change Rehearsal Halls

As a chorus becomes used to the peculiar acoustics of a rehearsal hall, they may find that their memories are jogged by certain ringing sounds or even by the decor of the room. Taking them out of these familiar surroundings removes these unknown crutches. Even before the last rehearsals, it is a good plan of attack to move them around to different surroundings. Each hall has a different set of acoustical properties, and with the changes the singers are forced to readjust their ears to hear themselves and the other singers in a new light. Borrow the band hall for a rehearsal, use the cafeteria (even if it sounds like you are singing inside a steel drum it is useful, since the singers must listen to new combinations of tones), go into the gymnasium, sing in the auditorium with the curtain open and closed, or even go out into an open field (with no reverberation at all they may hear the fundamental tones better and sing in tune more accurately). Such a simple thing as opening the windows may help, since this allows some sound to escape thus changing the reverberation characteristics. In the auditorium you can move the risers back and forth on the stage for new sound patterns, or you can even go out into the auditorium and sing as a group, or string the singers around the walls for some *real* separation. The object of all of this changing is to set up new relationships between the sections, the voices between each other, and the individual tones with each other. This forces the singers to adjust their ears and voices, and in the process they remove the old memory-joggers. If they cannot adjust readily, they are under-rehearsed.

Tryouts by Quartets

If you *really* want to find out who knows which pieces of music, have them sing by quartets unaccompanied. You will not have to listen to all of the singers to find out which sections are the weakest.

Sing for Any Group That Will Sit Still

There is no substitute for an audience. Until your singers are in front of an audience, you cannot be truly sure how they will react. A concert produces more adrenaline or less adrenaline, according to the size of the audience and the experience of the singers. When you are in the final throes of preparing a concert, try to invite some group—students from a study hall, another chorus, part of the band, teachers on a coffee break, anybody—to listen to ten or 15 minutes of singing. It does not have to be a full concert. Just a short burst of music without getting into robes or uniforms (although even this needs "rehearsal") will serve to find out how they sing under audience pressure and the stimulus of excitement. Sing for the PTA, the Ladies Aid, the Kiwanis Club, or a local junior high. Get them in front of an audience several times for ten- to 15-minute programs to drain off that nervousness which can undo many of the fine points you've drilled into them.

Record a Rehearsal

You are much too close to the chorus to make a completely valid judgment as to their fitness for a concert, or even for their exact position in the rehearsing of a new number. A tape recording helps you get outside of the directorial process so you can listen more objectively. You may have fallen into the habit of listening to only one or two sections of the chorus, and this is usually the section in which you sang when you were in a chorus. If your equipment is good enough, have your recording engineer set up the microphones so that two sections come out of one channel and two out of the other. This way you can isolate specific musical lines and not be distracted by other sections. Be hypercritical of everything, taking each line separately. Otherwise you may be lulled into a euphoria, thinking that "it's not as bad as I thought" when it actually may be.

The Visiting Fireman

One of the most effective and least used rehearsal techniques is the swapping out of duties with another choral conductor in a nearby school. You can say some things a dozen times to your students and still not get the results a visiting director can obtain with an offhand statement. Also, he will hear mistakes which you have overlooked. As you near the concert, it is valuable to get his or her judgment on the state of your choir, as well as the chance to sit out in the auditorium and listen to the sound, balance, and pronunciation.

Ensembles for Memorizing

In the final analysis, memorizing is one problem which can only be overcome by work. There are certain techniques which help (letting half of the chorus close the scores, for instance), but most memorizing comes with repetition. Instead of taking rehearsal time, assign each singer to an octet which is to work outside of class. Work out all of the notes and interpretations in class, but leave the memorizing of difficult passages to the small ensembles. Place one student in charge of the ensemble, and see that they do their work. Make them aware of the fact that you are going to check each voice before the next concert to see if they know their music.

181

With the preceding ten suggestions for testing your choir, you should be able to form a valid opinion as to its current standing in the rehearsing of a program. Because there always comes a time when you have made a mistake in programming too many pieces or works with too many problems, you will undoubtedly come to some concert less well-prepared than you would wish. Analysis cannot create time, but it can show you which pieces are in the best state of preparation so you will not waste time polishing what is already as shiny as it can become. As was stated in an earlier chapter, the conservation of rehearsal time is the name of the game.

Rehearsals and Warm-Ups on Tour

There will come a time when you will take a chorus on tour, either for several concerts or for a simple trip to a regional contest. In either case, you will have problems which will fall into two categories: (1) having some voice left in each student after the trip, and (2) polishing the voice that is left.

The tendency on the bus or car trip is to speak loudly enough to carry above the roar of the motor and the roar of other people talking. Remind your students that what they consider normal talking on the bus is actually a controlled shout. They must overcome the bus noises first, and then produce enough sound to communicate with a neighbor. A trip of an hour can knock an appreciable amount of brilliance off any voice, especially if that voice shouts continuously for the full hour.

When the bus stops, you will have certain problems in getting the singers unwound enough to have a profitable warm-up and rehearsal. Any new situation is cause for rejoicing by the average high school student, and a trip out of town is a fairly stimulating occurrence. The tour warm-up is almost the exact opposite of a normal warm-up, in that you need to choose your first exercises to calm the excited savages, not animate them. Take longer than usual to loosen the throat muscles. Have the singers hum a long, low note. Have them sing on the two sounds *aw* and *nn* (an open-lipped hum), alternating as in the following illustration.

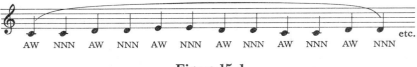

AW   NNN   AW   NNN   AW   NNN   AW   NNN   AW   NNN   AW   NNN   etc.

Figure 15–1

Emphasize to them that the muscles must be totally flaccid. Have them rub the muscles under and around their jaws and necks to get them untied.

These first warm-ups should be in the low part of their ranges. The muscles will already be tight enough from the bus ride. Your job is to loosen them up as much as possible. This does not apply to the muscles of the chest and waist areas. Here the idea is to get some muscle tone which has been ignored on the bus trip. Staccato singing, bending at the waist, and any other exercise which uses muscles below the throat area are valuable.

When the muscles are in the proper shape, begin working on a resonant tone. The choir's talking and ad-lib singing will probably have created a fuzzy edge on their voices. Nasal singing using the bright vowels *ee, eh,* and *aah* (as in *feet, bet,* and *grab*) may sound horrible, but it gets brilliance back into voices. Again, work on the lower range particularly. This is the tessitura which most beginning singers consider as requiring the least work. Actually, it takes the most physical labor and the sharpest ears to sing properly in the low part of the range. The following exercise emphasizes the lower range, as well as getting the perfect intervals in proper tuning.

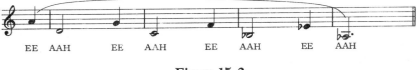

EE   AAH   EE   AAH   EE   AAH   EE   AAH

Figure 15–2

When the voices have been sufficiently revived, work on a few problem spots, but *don't go through a complete piece.* This has the effect of making the concert or contest anticlimactic. Even if one selection needs considerable work, it is best to take the

183

sections of the piece in reverse order to make the students think harder. Or take the entire work *pianissimo*. Again, the idea is to throw a different musical light on the work to make the students rethink the notes.

Dynamics and articulation can be handled on a "talk-through," during which you mention specific places where the chorus needs to be particularly careful but which they have normally performed correctly. It also helps to take a fast work very slowly in order to get the intonation readjusted to the new hall (if you can practice in the new hall), or to take a slow work quite fast to make them think through the entire melody. This is a good technique to use if they have all of the music memorized and only require some mental push-ups.

CHAPTER 16

Rehearsal Guide for
Five Choral Works

The purpose of this chapter is to take some of the suggestions presented in the first 15 chapters and apply them to specific problems in five different choral works from five different musical eras. Each of the works was chosen because of the number of separate problems contained therein. In each case we will determine what the composer was most interested in, what the separate problems are, and how they may be attacked. In some cases, this will mean giving a list of possibilities rather than a single solution. This is merely an acknowledgement that the abilities of choirs differ, just as the abilities of directors differ.

It may appear that the choir which will be performing the work in question is quite unlettered. We are only trying to cover all of the possibilities within reason for preplanning a rehearsal. Acts of nature such as sickness of a soloist or the heating plant bursting cannot be covered (this latter event happened to me once, knocking out an entire week of rehearsal). The reasoning behind each decision will be given unless such would be repetitious of previous lengthy explanations.

Renaissance Madrigal: "I Leave Thee (Mi Parto)," by Giaches de Wert*

One of the greatest problems with modern performance of Renaissance madrigals by high school groups (or any group, for that matter) is in getting enough emotion into the piece to fully realize the saccharine text. The phrase "I leave thee, ah, saddest parting!" is considerably more stilted to modern singers below voting age than the phrase "I'm for you, Bayeeeeeee-beee!" You may find that a brief illustrated lecture on the sweetness and gallantry of the Renaissance will help their understanding and acceptance, particularly if you emphasize that even then such sweetness was understood as artificial and surface emotion. If the students take the words seriously, they will destroy the effect. The delicate little pieces are just not able to carry that kind of profundity. Thomas Tomkins wrote in one of his madrigals "Ah, let me live for true love; ah, let me die for true love."

It may be necessary to have the singers speak the words several times before they get the correct attitude toward the performance of such texts. Ask them to overemote when they speak the text, using exaggerated inflections and extreme differences in volume. This should in all likelihood be the first element to work on. Get the singers interested in the *performance* (in a theatrical sense of the word) of the piece and you will have better cooperation in learning the notes. Finally, as the director you must exhibit more than just a toleration of this type of music. You must be enthusiastic and even excited about doing it. Until they understand the piece, you will have to supply the excitement. Without this enthusiasm your students may not believe it worthy of their time, or worse, that it is beneath their dignity and age.

What are the musical elements in this work? This is the first question you ask whenever you begin the analysis of a piece of music, whether it's written for chorus, stage band, or solo kazoo. In this work by Giaches de Wert the first thing to do is ignore the

---

* Wert, Giaches de. *I Leave Thee* (*Mi Parto*) (#60779), Belwin-Mills Publishing Corporation, Rockville Centre, N.Y. 11571, 1966. Used by permission.

interpretative marks, not because they are wrong but because they were not in the original manuscript. In this case they are quite good and can be followed in almost every instance, but since they were not there when the composer wrote the music, it is best to get a "clean" view of the piece. Look for specific voicings and combinations of voices.

The first thing you will notice is that Wert never used more than four voices at a time except at the final cadence. Why? So he could have contrast between sections, as between the first four measures which uses only the upper four voices and the next four measures which has the lower four voices on exactly the same music (transposed down a fifth) accompanying the Soprano I which has a solo part. This four-parts-accompanying-one-part remains until the final six measures when the texture thins to two or three voices accompanying the Soprano I. The reason for pointing this out is to emphasize the fact that the Soprano I must be treated as a solo, either for one person or as a section.

This problem of texture is almost all you can deduce from the music, except that all of the musical statements are very brief, usually less than a measure in length. This indicates that you will have to do a lot with the music in very short periods of time, particularly in view of the fact that the text is a hyperemotional one.

I   shall   die

Figure 16–1a

Measures 9 and 10 have the figure in various melodic shapes. It can be interpreted in the following four ways:

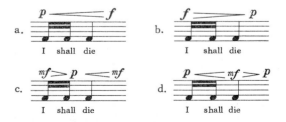

Figure 16–1b

187

as well as several more intricate styles using staccato notes to begin or end the motive. That does not mean any or all of these are correct, only that these are available and your job as conductor is to determine which one would be most effective in making the music and the text plain to the singers and the audience. My own preference is the last listed (part d) because it seems the most natural from a musical vantage point while remaining affected enough to be properly artificial. My next choice would be the one just before the last one (part c) because the word "I" is emphasized in the English translation, but not, of course, in the Italian original. This is a point to remember, that the language or translation may affect your choice of musical phrasing. There is no such thing as absolute musicianship, there is only a good, reasoned choice based on analysis and past experience with similar music. In Chapter 2, there was some emphasis given to color coding your conductor's score. You may need to put down two different concepts of the proper method of articulation or phrasing in a specific passage because you might need to experiment with different ideas to find the right one. Don't be afraid to tell your choir that you are experimenting with the music. Maybe one of them has an idea that will be better!

Since this particular piece has a translation, and since most high school choirs sing the English translation rather than the original text, you will need to examine the translation to see if there are places where you could improve the English text. Even if you do not know Italian or Latin or whatever, you still might find a place to reverse a pair of words to make the syllable accentuation more logical. You also might want to substitute a word to help the accentuation or to make the text less archaic. There is a set of choral works published in France with an English translation which was undoubtedly prepared by a Frenchwoman with no more than three months of Basic English under her belt. It is virtually unsingable because of the misplaced accents and obscure English words. My only choice was to perform them in French or scratch out a modified version of the printed English version. In this work by Wert the use of "thee" bothers me somewhat, so I would suggest experimenting using "you," which has the added benefit of coming much nearer to the final syllable of *parto* and *dolcissimo* than the bright *ee* vowel.

It may be that your chorus is so green that it cannot learn the parts in a full rehearsal. In this particular work, you might want to divide the singers into three groups: (1) the Soprano I by itself because it is a solo line, (2) the Soprano II and alto sections, and (3) the tenor and bass sections. Have section leaders chosen in advance with some brief suggestions as to the measures on which to concentrate. Allow them about 15 minutes, which means four or five minutes to get to the practice room and get organized, and ten minutes to work on the music. Since the piece is only about a minute and a half long, each group should get through it three or four times unless time is taken to pick out difficult parts. The next day you can have the altos and basses together, with the Soprano II and tenor sections in the practice room. By the third day the piece will fall together with ease. You have only used 15 minutes of two different rehearsals, and the work is under control.

There is another musicological note that is worth mentioning. The music of the sixteenth century often had instruments either doubling the vocalists or substituting for missing voice parts. If the Soprano I line is having trouble standing apart enough, try putting a flute, oboe, or clarinet with it. The added tone color will make it stand out in sharp relief. You will need to copy off the Soprano I line onto some score paper to eliminate the need for the flutist to turn pages. If you are of an experimental turn of mind, you might want to try substituting an instrument for each of the five vocal lines, then trying different combinations of two instruments and three vocal lines, or four instruments with a soloist. This might be made into a section of a concert, where the piece is played strictly as an instrumental solo, then with two or three different combinations of instruments and voices, and finally with voices only.

Places to watch for: *any time two voices form an interval of a fifth or an octave (or unison) call the singers' attention to it.* These are the basic intervals for tuning. In the first measure, the Soprano I and tenor sing G two octaves apart. The tenor line drops a fifth, which is always a danger point (they often drop too far) and the Soprano I is in the upper part of the range. Thus the pitches may be in tune with each other but flat in relation to the first chord. In the second measure, the tenor goes up to F which is already occupied an octave above by the Soprano I. An octave sung out of tune is a dreadful blight on the musical landscape. You may have to require these two parts to practice singing their lines as far as the first note of measure 5 because there are many strategically important intervals which must be clean before the piece will sing properly.

The "perfect" intervals of a fourth and fifth seem to be the intervals most often sung imperfectly, particularly by the bass and alto sections. Descending they go beyond the note and ascending they seem to miss just a bit getting there. This work has a very large number of such intervals in the lowest voice which happens to be singing at a specific time. In the first four measures, there are nine fourths or fifths in the tenor (the lowest voice). The next four measures have the bass singing the exact same part, except it is transposed a fifth lower. With this much emphasis on the perfect intervals, you would do well to make up a sight-reading sheet which utilizes the perfect intervals both melodically and in simple two-part harmony. Let them hear the "ring" of a perfectly tuned flawless interval. They may never have heard such an animal.

From a form standpoint it is important to call the students' attention to the similarity between the first four measures and the second four measures, the second being an exact transposition downward of the first four measures. The voicing becomes S-II/A/T/B. This is one method the composer used to get some unity in such a brief work while still having some variety. Since the voices are lower, there is a somewhat darker tone quality which you may wish to emphasize by having the singers sing more brightly on the first four measures and then cover their voices and sing more softly on the next four.

A similar job of alternating dynamics and/or tone qualities begins in measure 9 where the phrase "I shall die" is sung by two voices, then four voices, four voices, one voice, four voices, and a final four voices, all within a space of two-and-a-half measures. Obviously, you cannot sing all of them at the same dynamic level or the whole passage loses its musicality and becomes merely a sequence of bland chords. Try speaking the phrase "I shall die" six straight times to see the problem of sameness. Setting such sameness to music does not entirely relieve the problem. In speaking these six repetitions, you may find the key to the interpretation. It may go in the following manner :

Figure 16–1c

This interpretation would utilize the difference in texture and intensity between a single section singing *forte* and without harmony, and four sections singing harmony very softly. The number of decibels on a loudness scale might be the same, but the effect would be quite different.

The relative loudness of each repetition of "I shall die" depends to some extent on how you phrase the three notes (see Figure 16–1b). It has been stated before and will continue to be repeated: *there is no one, final way to phrase or interpret any musical passage.* Choruses with greater or less ability, the size of the chorus, the room in which it is being performed—all of these affect the interpretation of a work.

Baroque Cantata: J. S. Bach, "Cantata No. 140"

The apparent sameness of a piece of music from the Baroque era often hides many problems. The so-called "walking bass" and a constant stream of repetitions of melodic fragments can blur the fact that much contrast is available, and that these contrasts must be made plain both to the performers and to the audience before the music is successful.

J. S. Bach's Cantata No. 140, *Wachet auf, ruft uns die Stimme* ("Sleepers Wake") operates on at least four different musical levels. This is not as complicated as it might sound, since two of these levels are instrumental and two are vocal. As with all music, first isolate the elements, then figure the best manner in which to make them plain.

We will assume for the beginning of the analysis that you do not have a full orchestra. In this Bach work you would need only two oboes, an English horn, two violins, a viola and cello, and/or string bass with the keyboard instrument for the continuo part. Since these instruments are not always readily available in every high school, our first analysis will have to do with as simple an accompaniment as possible.

The first view of the full score shows the instruments playing 16 measures before the voices enter. The two musical elements consist of a dotted rhythm figure in the first four measures which alternates between the strings and the woodwinds. In the piano/organ reduction of the vocal score this is shown as one continuous line of dotted eighths and sixteenths when actually it is antiphonal writing between strings and winds. This is a fundamental reason for having the full orchestral score for the analysis of the work even though you will be using only a single keyboard instrument for the actual rehearsals and performance. Unless you know what went on in the composer's mind, you cannot do a decent job of recreating it. In this particular work, it would help if you could get an organ with two manuals and an organist with enough facility to perform the work as it was intended. The organ score would look like this for the first four measures:

Figure 16–2a

This would not require much hand dexterity but the feet would have to be fairly well trained, particularly when the dotted rhythm is transferred to the continuo line in measure 5 (Figure 16–2b).

Figure 16–2b

There is another solution to the problem of making the antiphonal effect more pronounced. You might consider using two pianos with two accompanists, one on each side of the chorus. One could play the woodwind parts, the other could play the string parts. This would allow the music to be played in the same octave as it was originally written while bringing out the proper antiphonal effect. It would also allow you to use at least one pianist with limited ability, since playing only the oboe and English horn parts would not be overly complicated. It would probably not be a good idea to alternate octaves on a piano to show the two different timbres. This is a different musical effect and should be used only as a last resort.

Measure 5 is also the beginning of the second musical element, a little "springboard" melodic fragment which, like the opening dotted rhythm element, is used antiphonally between the strings and the winds.

Figure 16–2c

These are not on the same notes but in different parts of the octave, so there is not as much of a problem of obscuring this antiphonal effect in the music writing.

The bass/continuo line, with its dotted-rhythm pattern in

193

measures 5–8 and 13–16 must be made to stand out against the sixteenth-note pattern in the upper instruments. With a piano this is not a great problem, since the attack on each repeated note makes an accent loud enough to be heard. The organ is another matter. The notes must be played staccato or they will become only a mildly articulated blur. One solution to this is to do what the musicians of the seventeenth and eighteenth centuries would have done, put a cello or string bass on the line and have it play highly articulated notes, possibly even pizzicato. Your "instrumental ensemble" might logically consist of a string bass and an organ, which would give a highly satisfactory musical presentation of this work. Bach, himself, was not averse to substituting instruments when he happened to find himself without certain ones. The choral conductor in a school with limited resources should consider the Baroque era a treasure-house of material for adaptation (within stylistic guidelines, to be sure). One fine musicologist found himself performing a Bach cantata without a Baroque trumpet and with no regular trumpeter capable of negotiating the intricate patterns of the music. He found that a soprano saxophone played by a musician with taste substituted excellently, gave almost the same sound, and was considerably easier to obtain. The rule is: *find what the composer wanted, then make reasoned substitutions.*

In the matter of conducting an instrumental ensemble, you should not consider a plurality of stringed instruments on each part a necessity. A soloist of decent ability on each part is sufficient, unless you have a chorus of 60 or 70 voices. Keep the chorus down to a moderate size so the voices and instruments can balance without one or the other having to overblow or hold back unnaturally. From an acoustical standpoint, two violins are less than one-fourth louder than a single violin, and adding a third violin raises the perceived loudness by less than 50 per cent over the single violin. The only thing to be changed appreciably is the texture of the sound, plus the intonation problems of getting three instruments to blend on fast passages.

Since good oboeists are more scarce than good tenors in the average high school, and English horns are virtually nonexistent, you will probably have to substitute for these instruments. As we have seen, Bach wanted three contrasting musical sounds (strings, woodwinds, and voices), so substituting clarinets for the oboes and the English horn would still fulfill his musical wishes to a degree, and clarinets are considerably easier to find.

The two musical elements in the vocal parts are: (1) the *cantus firmus* sung throughout by the sopranos,

Figure 16-2d

and (2) the accompanying figure in the lower three voices, which is usually an echo effect with pyramiding entrances. The basis of the movement is Otto Nicolai's famous hymn first published in 1599. Because of the nature of the musical embroidery in the accompanying parts, it would be easy to allow the simple melody to be obscured by the musical busy work. The first problem is to determine how the soprano part is to remain clearly "in sight." When first performed it would have been sung by boy sopranos, which would have given the sound enough contrast with the surrounding lines of music to remain visible. As the conductor, you will need to work with the tone quality to give it an "edge" similar to the sound of a group of boy sopranos. It is unwise to overload the section just to keep the soprano part in the foreground.

Another solution would be to use contrasting articulations on the vocal lines. This would entail having the soprano line with its cantus firmus sung legato while the accompanying lines are sung with light accents, not staccato but with each note clearly heard. These alto, tenor, and bass parts would not be sung as loudly as the soprano melody, but the accents would still make the lines clean and solidly heard. In a passage such as shown in Figure 16-2e, all four of the basic musical elements of this work would be easily perceived by even the most unlettered listener.

It is obvious from this illustration that *blend* is a word with two meanings. It can mean a unity of sound within a section, or it can mean a unity of sound between two or more sections. In the

Figure 16–2e

passage in Figure 16–2e, there obviously must be one basic sound
within the soprano section. However, the sopranos should not
blend, in the normal use of the term, with the lower three sections
since the sopranos have different musical requirements which keep
them separate. On the other hand, the lower three parts should
have a blend (a similarity of timbres), since the music is similar
in texture. In the first two measures, there are only harmonic
chords, with the individual voices meaning nothing from a melodic standpoint. Following these two chords the basses, altos, and
tenors come in on successive beats with similar polyphonic material, which by the very nature of its melodic contour makes each
section stand out. Articulation on the polyphonic sections, blend-

196

ing on the harmonic sections, and a separate timbre for the soprano line takes care of the vocal musical requirements.

You may find it useful to have everyone sing first one part, then the next, in order to show the various musical elements. The soprano part will not be a problem, except to keep the singers from rushing or dragging. The sameness of the soprano line may lull them into sloppy singing. To counteract this, have them sing the line as if it were composed of eighth notes with staccato markings:

wa (ah) (ah) (ah) (ah) (ah)   chet (eh) (eh) (eh) (eh) (et)   auf (ah) (ah) (ah) (ah) (auf)

Figure 16–2f

This makes them aware of the underlying eighth-note pulse. When they can sing this without slowing down or speeding up, let them sing it as if the eighth notes were slurred (with a slight impulse, but still legato and connected). When they are singing the final rehearsals and during the concert they should still hear the eighth-note rhythm in their minds. Even the lower three parts should have this awareness of the eighth-note rhythm. Just because the time signature happens to be ¾ is no reason to consider a quarter note as the fundamental pulse unit. In some instances, for example in the dotted rhythm shown in Figures 16–2a and 16-2b, the basic beat is the sixteenth note. Unless the singers and instrumentalists understand this fact, the dotted rhythm will tend to blur into a triplet figure and the sopranos singing the *cantus firmus* will rush or slow the tempo.

Figure 16–2g

Figure 16–2h

Figure 16–2i

One problem you will probably run into will be the hanging over on some notes by certain sections in an unconscious attempt to match the length of notes in other sections. In *Wachet auf* this occurs at the end of virtually every vocal section.

Figure 16–2g would not be as great a problem as 2h or 2i because there is an obvious difference between the length of the soprano note and the final notes of the other two sections. In 2h and 2i, the singers may try to "even up" the notes so everyone stops together. Calling their attention to the problem will help some, but if this does not tidy up the individual cutoffs you will need to take the lower three sections as a unit and get them right. Have them sing all the notes of the phrase (including quarter notes) as eighth notes, either staccato or "quasi-staccato" (an accented legato) as in Figure 16–2j.

This can be done with either the words, as in the illustration, where the syllables on the quarter notes are simply repeated, or the singers can do the same thing on a neutral syllable such as *la* or *ta*. Using the text and dividing the syllables on quarter notes is more effective since it illustrates the problem more accurately. The singers quickly realize that a quarter consists of only two eighth notes, and the tone is to stop after the second eighth note. It is obvious that this technique will work with any choral music, not just with Baroque cantatas.

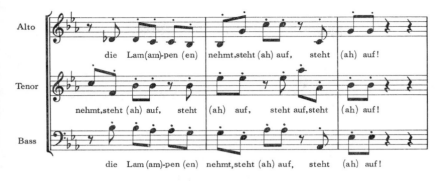

Figure 16–2j

In measure 135, the lower three voices have an intricate, lengthy sixteenth-note introduction on the word "Alleluia." This uses the musical material from the instrumental accompaniment shown in Figure 16-2c, which should make it easier for the chorus to hear the rhythmic figure. In long passages using basically the same note values, inexperienced choruses have a tendency to either drag or rush, particularly the latter. In a passage such as Figure 16-2k, have them sing the entire line on *ta* (a more exact and crisp beginning sound than *la* and constricts the throat less than *da*), and if possible have them snap their fingers on the beginnings of each fundamental beat (indicated by ↓).

Figure 16–2k

This keeps the beat lively while the hand movement of snapping the fingers acts as a metronome. In actual performance, the continuo line will take the place of the finger snapping since the bass line is a series of ♪ ૪ ♪ ૪ ♪ ૪ measures.

199

Early Nineteenth Century: "Elegy," by L. v. Beethoven

The first item, as always, is to find what the composer used in his composition. Until we know the elements of the piece, we cannot begin proper rehearsing. The outline of the form of Beethoven's *Elegy*, Op. 118, is as follows:

21 measures—instrumental introduction
12   "   —homophonic choral
10   "   —fugal, ending homophonic
10   "   —fugal, similar to above section
6   "   —quasi-polyphonic
4   "   —instrumental interlude, using opening material
14   "   —homophonic, using opening material
8   "   —quasi-polyphonic, ending homophonic, unaccompanied
2   "   —instrumental postlude

Homophonic and polyphonic writing have different requirements, the former having problems of blend of voices, and the latter having problems of separation of voices. Fortunately, by the time of Beethoven, composers were using more written instructions on the proper realization of their music. These included such phrases as *sotto voce* (literally "under the voice," or a subdued tone) and *langsam und sanft* (slow and soft), as well as written dynamics for all voices and instrumental entrances. However, this is not as much help as might be expected, since *forte* means loud but it doesn't say how loud or how many singers to use. Also "slow and soft" does not say how slow or how soft the music is to be played or sung. Because of this incompleteness of the score you, as the director, will have to make some value judgments.

This work was originally written for four vocal soloists and a string quartet. It has been performed with a chorus and either a string quartet or a string ensemble. Both performance methods work equally well, except that having eight or ten sopranos sing the soprano line makes a richer and mushier tone than when one good soloist sings the notes. In the homophonic writing this is fine, but in the polyphonic writing you will have to work more on pronunciation and articulation to make each voice part visible. On the other hand, the solo voices may have problems blending on the chordal passages. If you have soloists perform the piece, you will need to emphasize that their accustomed tone may have to be modified to balance and blend with the other soloists.

The instrumental accompaniment must be thought of as two separate problems, depending on whether you use a piano or strings in the performance. With the piano your main problem will be to make the tone as legato as possible, keeping the percussive effect under the vocal sound. The sound of piano hammers hitting strings is considerably different than bows playing across strings, particularly in the fugal portions. In the softest passages, the piano should just barely be heard. This will set the scene for the voices and keep them from clobbering the *sotto voce* sections.

If you happen to have some string players, you will run into different problems. This is an excellent work for high school string players since the range is not extreme, the tempo is moderate, and the writing is interesting. On the other hand, there are some problems of intonation which have been obvious in every performance I have either conducted or heard. The opening three measures are as bad as any in the entire piece, possibly because the strings have to enter very softly and slowly. It will take some work to get them in tune, so don't leave the rehearsing of the introduction until the final rehearsal. Also, in measure 14, the Violin I has an ascending scale passage which just ends on an almost unheard note. It takes a few times through this passage by high school string players before they get the idea of a proper diminuendo.

At the point where the voices enter, the strings are playing eighth notes. There will be a tendency to play either very short, staccato notes or to make the second eighth note into a quarter note. Be sure the singers make each note exactly an eighth followed by exact eighth rests. In measure 52 there is a five-beat diminuendo in both voices and strings, ending in a chord resolution. Make sure neither group plays the chord of resolution too loudly. The tendency is to accent the chord that finishes the resolution, possibly because it is a predictable sound, but this is precisely the reason it should *not* be emphasized. A rule which is usually applicable is: *bring out the unusual and nonpredictable sounds; de-emphasize the sounds which are expected.*

The final measure in the instruments also creates problems, again because it is slow and soft, and also the lower three instruments are in their lowest register.

In the vocal lines, a major problem will be in phrasing and shaping short series of notes. The opening notes will serve as examples:

Figure 16–3a

All three of the phrasing possibilities might work under varying conditions of the text. In this case, (A) would probably not work because there would be a loss of intensity across the comma in the text which would indicate that the second chord was some kind of resolution or phrase ending, and it most obviously is neither of these. Either (B) or (C) might work, and here the ability of your choir may dictate the extent of the musicality you demand. If the singers cannot control the crescendos and diminuendos of (C) you might be forced to use (B), which is not a bad interpretation, just not as thorough as (C).

Your problem will be in getting the singers to diminuendo smoothly and not in steps. Since smooth phrasing and even changes of volume are absolute necessities, you may want to write out simple exercises with extreme phrasing requirements. Something like the following exercise, when performed exactly as indicated, will open up all kinds of musical possibilities and make the singers aware of the actual work, both mental and physical, that goes into a good choral performance.

However, you must follow the dynamics of the exercise pre-

Figure 16–3b

cisely or there is little reason to use it. The dynamic change must not hang over into another beat but must begin and end exactly where it is specified. In addition, the change must be smooth. To facilitate smoothness have them sing one note, going from *pianissimo* to *fortissimo* in eight slow beats and, without taking a breath, coming smoothly back to *pianissimo*. Most choruses crescendo fairly well but the return to *pp* consists of a huge drop to about *mp* and then a gradual loss of intensity. The intensity and resonance must stay the same throughout the exercise, or you must consider it incorrectly sung. Remember the axiom: *unless a singer can crescendo and diminuendo smoothly on a note without changing the timbre or the pitch, that note is not under control.*

Most high school singers will not want to work hard enough to realize dynamics as extreme as you will want. As much as anything, they will think such extremes are silly and affected. Pop musicians have few such subtleties of musicianship, except in the performances by established artists performing solo material. One method of explaining the problem and necessity of such is to play the singers a recording of a string quartet or string ensemble work with a slow movement. It will take some close listening, much closer than most of them are used to, but eventually many of them will get the message.

Back to Beethoven. Since Beethoven was pragmatic enough in 1814 to realize that fugal music needed more instrumental support than did harmonic writing, he thoughtfully allowed the instruments to double the voices in polyphonic sections. This cuts down on some of the problems of singing the exact notes, but it does not entirely eliminate the intonation hassle. Until

203

the singers can perform the fugal portions (all relatively brief) unaccompanied, they do not really have control of their parts. While learning the parts, have the accompanist play the notes staccato and fairly softly. Also, playing in another octave when working with only one or two sections helps. The volume of the piano-playing parts should be enough to tell the singers they are either on or off the proper note but not enough to overpower the voices.

On the other hand, there are passages which have block harmonies in the voices and an accompaniment of only block chords in the instruments. In measure 48, the piano reduction has only one chord sounding through three beats. With strings the sound would stay at the same level throughout the measure, but with a piano the tone decays fairly rapidly. In this case, you might tell the accompanist to play a series of eighth notes to reiterate the pitches. If the singers are singing *forte* or *fortissimo* they might miss the initial attack of the piano tone and continue through the entire chord out of tune.

At the return of the A section (measure 61), the bass entrance is somewhat awkward with a C-sharp against the tenor and soprano B. Since the bass line is doubled by the cello line, have the accompanist play the cello's notes (lowest notes of the left hand) until the basses have it memorized (you might want them to sing it on *la* or *ta*). The basses will have no trouble "hearing" their note before they sing it if they learn it in this manner.

Beginning in measure 68, the entrances and cutoffs of the music become less predictable. Before this they follow a more or less anticipated rhythmic scheme, but suddenly Beethoven throws in the following passage:

Figure 16–3c

The rhythmic sequence is totally out of context with what has gone before, which means the singers will need to shift gears mentally in order to get the rhythm, pitch, and dynamic indications correct. You may have to resort to the device of their singing everything in eighth-note rhythm to force them to hold the dotted half note in measure 68 to the beginning of the next measure, and then in measure 72 to keep them from drifting past the allotted time of the half note in an unconscious attempt to mirror the dotted note in measure 68.

Another problem in this passage is in the abrupt dynamics and one ambiguous indication of a dynamic level. Sudden *forte* and *piano* markings usually indicate some theatrical effects are desired. Don't allow your singers to substitute *mezzo-forte* and *mezzo-piano* for true *forte* and *piano* levels.

The ambiguous indication is in measures 71 and 72, where the eighth note appears to be *piano* and the half note *forte*. Such an abrupt change within the context of a two-note phrase would be out of keeping with the style which had been set up in the earlier part of the work. Possibly both notes should be *forte*, or more likely the first note should be *mezzo-forte* crescendoing to *forte*.

This same passage has a tuning problem. Measures 68 and 69 have the soprano line skipping down by a seventh into a dissonant interval with the altos. Whenever you have a dissonant interval between two voices in music of this style, analyze the rest of the voices to see how the chord structure is designed. Music written before the twentieth century was usually based on triads or extensions of the triad (sevenths, ninths). When you find voices with the interval of a second, you are usually going to find a seventh chord or ninth cord of some denomination, often involving a suspension or anticipation. When this happens, eliminate the voice which contains the seventh or ninth of the chord. This keeps the triadic feeling so the remaining voices can find the notes, but the troublesome dissonance is temporarily omitted. In this passage, just have the altos drop out in measures 69 and 70 until the other voices are secure on their pitches. Since the alto line moves only by a second, there is little problem in learning their part. However, if there is a problem you can use the same procedure as above, only the soprano drops out. Going into this passage is not a problem since the instruments cue the voices sufficiently so that the F-sharp seventh chord will tune fairly fast.

Folk Song Arrangement: Brahms: "Awake, Awake" *

Arrangements of folk songs are not crumbs to be thrown to the masses as a sop to keep them quiet. In the hands of a fine musician, arrangements of traditional material can become art works in their own right. Your job as a musician is to choose only those arrangements which exhibit good craftsmanship and not just a smooth, bland flow of notes with a familiar tune.

Brahms was one of the earliest collectors and arrangers of folk material. Some are simple harmonizations, some are intricate polyphonic compositions with the folk tune as merely a point of departure. "Awake, Awake" is relatively intricate for a folk tune arrangement. As with all works, your first job is to take it apart and list the various musical elements.

The first thing you will find is that the eighth-note rhythm is constant throughout the piece. At almost any given instant, somebody is singing a separate syllable on an eighth note. This puts a strain on the singers, since they must mold their phrases within the confines of a steady eighth-note pulse. Further, the entrances must be clearly heard. Thus, at the very first entrance the singers must be in control of the vocal line; otherwise, the bass line will not get out of the way of the soprano and tenor entrances (Figure 16–4a).

This may seem like fussy detail but we are speaking of proper musicianship and not just sound. In fact, the first five measures in the bass line should be phrased as shown in Figure 16–4b.

There are some relatively abrupt dynamic changes in measures 10 and 11 and also in measure 13 (Figure 16–4c).

---

* Johannes Brahms. *Six Folk Songs.* Copyright, Edward B. Marks Music Corporation. New York: 1948. Used by permission.

Figure 16–4a

Figure 16–4b

Figure 16–4c

The problem is to keep the diminuendo from sounding like a *subito piano*. You may find that you will have to work out a special exercise to get the concept over to the singers. It sounds ridiculous, but the use of words often confuses singers and gives an artificial sound to the vocal line *as heard by the singers themselves*. Something like the following exercise can help young singers learn to differentiate between a true *piano* and merely *mezzo-piano*.

Figure 16–4d

The problem is that singers hear the volume or explosiveness of the consonants and judge loudness by these; whereas, the true volume (as perceived by the audience and the director) comes from the vowel sound.

A diminuendo at a phrase ending is relatively simple if the voice part goes down, but an ascending vocal line seems to mean "louder" to many singers. This is particularly true with a skip of a fourth or more. The bass line at the cadence of the first section has the basses skipping up by a fourth:

Figure 16–4e

Because of this movement, the basses will need to backpedal more than the other parts. Going upward in pitch increases the intensity so the basses will have to overcome this effect as well as the natural desire to sing louder. Otherwise, it will appear that the basses have accented the final chord when actually the sound should almost disappear.

In the entire 45 measures of the work, there is only one accidental, and that is a simple passing tone in the third measure from the end. Obviously there is a great need for the singers to understand where the notches in the diatonic scale are located, particularly in the skips within the tonic chord. This entire piece works well for an exercise in diatonic sight-reading. Have the entire chorus sing each line, transposing downward or upward to suit the voices. My own favorite method is to sing it with numbers, then with solfege syllables, then on *la*. A variation of this, and a bit more difficult, is to sing it with numbers (or syllables) two parts at a time, with all of the men on one part and all of the women on another part. This is hardly to be considered time wasted since any sight-reading training is valuable, and if you are also learning a concert number you are so much the richer. As much as possible use your basically diatonic works for this type of sight-reading practice.

Choral writing which is almost totally diatonic has a built-in danger, and that is that the singers will get sloppy about their intonation. The sight-reading mentioned above is designed to help solve this problem. Another cure is to move the pitch around so the students never rely on muscle memory instead of ear-training for proper note selection. Singing by muscle memory is an unconscious type of singing where notes are sung which are close to the pitch but not quite on the exact pitch. Moving the pitch up a half tone or down a half tone keeps the students from relying on muscle tension for accurate intonation.

Because of this intonation problem, you might want to use a staccato technique for trueing up the notes. Have the entire chorus sing each note staccato. With this style of singing, they will have to sing the note correctly immediately and not wait until the tone is established before tuning it. You may have to sing the work at half-tempo to give the singers more time to adjust mentally to the different pitches, especially during early rehearsals. This is one of those pieces which is relatively easy during early rehearsals but extremely trying during the final polishing. You might want to use this work, and others like it, as tryout pieces for your grading period. Have the students sing in quartets to check on their sense of blend and intonation.

Since this is a folk song arrangement, and not a more austere piece of concert literature, the text can have a different approach to pronunciation. In most concert pieces the vowel sounds are kept as pure as possible; that is, diphthong sounds are sung on one or the other of the vowel sounds instead of gradually changing the vowel through the length of the note. In this arrangement, none of the syllables are held for an appreciably long time. Work on a pronunciation that is nearer to a spoken pronunciation. In fact, it might help to have them speak the soprano line so you can check their pronunciation for regionalisms or stilted accentuations. It is also a help to have each section pronounce its own line by itself to enable you to check more carefully. Due to different levels of maturity, the pronunciation of the women's sections might be better than that of the men's sections.

The actual interpretation is fairly well encased within the constant eighth-note rhythm and the indicated dynamics. However, at the end of the work there is an indicated ritardando and a concluding two measures of *forte*.

Figure 16–4f

In order to give the piece a more positive ending, you might wish to insert a brief hold on the word "earth," then an *a tempo* for the final phrase of "O never, never leave me!" Notice that the final note is only an eighth note, and there is no fermata or other device for lengthening it. Extending the word "earth" (in the next-to-last phrase) or the final word "me" unduly, might force the piece into a different style for that one section and thus make it a false interpretation. There is an ever-present danger in the additions a conductor makes to a score. The new elements may be in a different style or they may warp a small song into a pseudo-big style. This has often been done with folk song arrangements, Bach chorale settings, and other choral works with relatively simple textures.

Contemporary: "Comrade! Brother!" by Jack Boyd[1]

Because contemporary music has all of the musical devices from the past eight centuries from which to draw inspiration, all of the problems listed in the earlier parts of this chapter will apply to contemporary choral writing, plus some that are new and unique. Melodies that skip into dissonances, chords with six or eight separate members, rapid articulation and dynamic changes, as well as nonvocal sounds and nonnotated tone clusters all present new choral music problems which have been encountered before but not in such profusion or in such combinations.

The piece of music here analyzed was chosen because it illustrated more problems in a shorter space of time than any other single piece of music, while remaining within the technical ability of a high school choir (I've directed high school choirs which performed this work).

The first order of business in the rehearsal of a work with this type of text is to read and discuss the poem. If possible, get other poetry of Stephen Crane (the author of this particular text) and show that his style of word writing is highly condensed, and hence the music is also highly condensed to stay in the same style. The words themselves suggest certain rhythms. To illustrate this to your students have them speak the entire text. The phrase ". . . many devils, running, leaping . . ." has a set of two-syllable words which produces a percussive effect, like a snare drum pattern.[2]

---

[1] Jack Boyd. "Comrade! Brother!" © Copyright 1968 by G. Schirmer, Inc., New York. Used by permission.

[2] There is a companion work to this piece printed by the same publisher, the text of which might be read at the same time.

The fragmentation of a word into its component sounds draws the singers' and the audience's attention to the number of available noises which must be sounded before the word is completed. On the third measure, the word "place" is divided into its three sounds and combined with the word "high." The problem here is to obtain and hold the pure sounds of *ah* in *high,* the *l* sound in *place,* the long *a* in *place* and the final short hissing sound at the end of *place.* The sound should be almost instrumental, and should not be "diphthongized" in any way. It is relatively slow, so there should be no problem of finding the pitches, particularly since the soprano section gives the basic pitches in the first two measures. Notice, however, that the opening *mezzo-forte* is reduced to *piano* for the word fragmentation. The singers will undoubtedly get louder when they sing this fragmented word in an attempt to hear themselves and their section. Contrary to their efforts, the softer they sing the easier it is to hear the parts. A loud, forced tone usually creates a vibrato or wobble of some kind; whereas, a well-constructed, soft tone straightens out such problems. Emphasize to the singers that they are to sound like woodwinds and not voices.

This emphasis on the instrumental quality of the voices is particularly important in measures 6 and 7 where the fragmented word accompanies the jagged melody on "many devils, running, leaping." The contrast between the straight tone of the women's voices and the angular, sharply articulated men's line should be emphasized.

Since there are problems in singing the words "many devils, running, leaping" rapidly, you should begin by having the entire chorus speak the words slowly, distinctly, and with every sound in every word present. As you increase the tempo, there will be a tendency to drop some sounds. There is no shortcut in learning to speak and then sing the words; the only solution is repeated articulation of every sound. The "ing" sound in "running" and "leaping" will be the first to mutate into "runnin'" and "leapin'." In areas of the country where a lazy drawl is a way of life, you will experience problems with lips which almost refuse to move that fast. They will not be able to assimilate your instructions in one rehearsal. Be sure that each sixteenth note is exact. The phrase should sound like a snare drum pattern.

The phrase "leaping and carousing" has the rhythmic pattern of:

leap - ing   and   ca - rous - ing

Figure 16–5a

The singers will want to make the last pair of eighth notes (on "rousing") into a dotted rhythm to match the previous beat. While you *could* perform it in this manner, may I say that if the composer had wanted that particular rhythm, he would probably have written it so. Fidelity to the score and tidying up small mistakes is the beginning of wisdom, chorally speaking.

The five measures which use the word "sin" is a tricky passage because the sibilant is emphasized in the men's voices while the hummed *nn* sound is emphasized in the women's voices. The women's parts should not cause much trouble since the word is actually "ssnn," with the vowel all but ignored. The indication in the score is for the women to sing their notes with an accent, then glissando downward for the remainder of the measure on the *nn* sound. It may take the singers some time to learn the glissando, so begin by singing only the notes on *nn*, but with the proper accents. Then have them do the glissando. If your singers are of average ability, they will move downward about a minor third the first few times; whereas, the score shows a drop of about an octave. The indication in the score for the tempo is "very fast," which is actually much easier than trying to do the same thing slowly. Performed rapidly, the singers will worry only about the first note, while sung slowly the individual pitches may tend to appear.

The men singing the word "sin" is an entirely different problem, due to the exploded *ss* sound on the third beat of each measure. This problem is compounded by the very fast tempo and the necessity of getting the interval of a fifth or fourth between the tenor and bass lines exactly in tune. Start with either the words or the intervals, but whichever you start with get that part right before you complicate matters with the other. It would probably be best to get the intervals in tune first since this will be the most obvious mistake to the audience. Have the singers sing the pure vowel in "sin" while they learn the notes. The "brighter" vowels of *ih* (short *i*) and *ee* (long *e*) are the best for tuning. The darker, more covered sounds of *ah, oh,* or *oo* are not as useful in this respect. The use of *ih* was chosen because it is the same as the vowel in "sin," so the singers will be getting used to the tuning of that vowel.

When the men have their lines together, put them with the women's parts on a single vowel but still without the *s* and the *n* sounds. At this point, the singers may still have trouble getting their parts. If this sort of mild dissonance is still beyond them, separate the sections by sending each voice part into a different corner of the rehearsal room. If even this is not enough separation, assign a different vowel sound to each of the four sections so there will be less overlap in timbres.

Just getting this section in tune may be enough of a problem for one rehearsal if your chorus is relatively new at such music. Do not push such music the first few rehearsals. Ten minutes a day is enough until the singers begin identifying with the style (they will eventually, but it takes time). When the notes are in tune, you can start working the tenor and bass lines on their percussive rhythm on "sin." The *ss* sound must be exploded on the third beat of the measure instead of the first beat as in the women's parts. You may need to slow the tempo drastically in order to get this correctly pronounced. This contrasts with the women's parts which benefited from a fast tempo. Further, the men will have to hit their pitches correctly after the long (relatively long) sibilant sound. Try working on this particular problem at the beginning of a day's rehearsal of this work. Reading this sort of music at sight is almost out of the question for high school students. It is a type of theatre music which, like the theatre itself, requires some living with to fully understand.

Although the passage in the following illustration is notated thus (Figure 16–5b),

Figure 16–5b

there is a tendency to sing it in this manner:

Figure 16–5c

A long glissando is difficult for amateur singers to time. Most of them want to hold on to the notes until the last instant and then slide very quickly to the next note. The proper method is to begin sliding as soon as the tone is established. There are no tricks to get this accomplished; you just work with them until they do it.

One note here about pronunciation: *there is a tendency in many parts of the nation to add or subtract extra syllables in words.* It is this addition or subtraction of sounds that gives us our regional dialects. One problem is the changing of an *eh* sound (as in *pen*) into an *aah* vowel sound (as in *pan*). A sound which is often added to words is an *uh* vowel after the brighter vowels *ee, ih, eh,* and *aah* (as in *bee, zip, bed,* and *sand*). Northern dialects are rampant with such words as "bee-uh-skit-ball" instead of "basketball" and "ih-ut" for "it." In this piece of music, the word "grinning" is extended in time to cover four beats, which means the singers have more time to add this extra *uh* sound. Since most of the singers who speak in this manner will not be aware that they do so (owners of dialects seldom realize their ownership), it will take some time to show them what is occurring. You will probably have to start with a pure *ih* vowel held for a considerable length of time and then stopped without the addition of *uh*. When your singers can do this properly, have them do the *ih* with a concluding *nn* sound, and then go back and forth between the *ih* vowel and the *nn* using only the tip of the tongue to obtain the *nn* sound. To get the *uh* they will have to adjust the middle of the tongue. Also, watch that the lips do not change shape. When the *ih* and *nn* sounds have been learned satisfactorily, you can add any beginning consonant and the sound should remain constant.

The final passage is not as complicated as it might appear at first glance. The soprano and alto lines have the descending sequence of intervals of a fourth or fifth used by the men a few measures before. Meanwhile, the men's voices take the same pitches sung by the women and the same dynamics, except they have a downward glissando into a spoken final syllable. Because of this spoken final syllable, you may need to tell the tenors and basses that no two voices are to wind up on the same pitch, although they start on the same pitch. This concept of different pitches within the same section will be new to some of them and you will need to watch that they do not polarize on one pitch. At first you may need to work the entire four measures without the glissando until the pitches are firmly in their minds, and then add the nonpitched sounds. At the final polishing, try the men without the women and see if they know the pitches without the cueing of the treble voices.

Because this work is so sectional you will need to rehearse in reverse several times; that is, sing the final section, then the final two sections, then the final three sections, etc. This emphasizes the last section and makes sure the chorus is going toward familiar material. In a difficult or unusual work, the choir may work on the earlier sections to the detriment of the last parts. Rehearsing in reverse gives them the needed work on the last sections.

A final admonition: *sing the notes as they are written*. When there is an eighth note, be sure the singers perform an eighth note and not a dotted quarter just because they like the sound or because it is easier (which means: requires less thought and technique). The opening passage by the soprano section is as follows:

I   stood   up - on   a   high   place,

Figure 16–5d

The last note is an eighth note. Singing "place" on an eighth note gives emphasis to the consonants and the final sibilant. This is the style of the work. Lengthening the note to emphasize the vowel sound would not be the same effect or the same style. Consistency of style is one of the fundamental problems in any type of music.

Index

LINCOLN CHRISTIAN COLLEGE AND SEMINARY